WITH THE
# 11th (H.A.C.) REGIMENT, R.H.A.
IN WORLD WAR II.

1537  1945

# WITH THE
# 11th (H.A.C.) REGIMENT, R.H.A.
## IN WORLD WAR II.

*By*

MAJOR KENNETH BOLTON, M.C.

The Naval & Military Press Ltd

*Published by*

**The Naval & Military Press Ltd**
Unit 5 Riverside, Brambleside
Bellbrook Industrial Estate
Uckfield, East Sussex
TN22 1QQ England

Tel: +44 (0)1825 749494

www.naval-military-press.com
www.nmarchive.com

*In reprinting in facsimile from the original, any imperfections are inevitably reproduced and the quality may fall short of modern type and cartographic standards.*

# PREFACE

This brief summary of the history of the 11th (H.A.C.) Regiment, R.H.A., has been compiled from Regimental and Battery War Diaries and from narratives supplied by members of the Regiment. Records of the early days in the Western Desert are incomplete and the fighting at El Agheila and Knightsbridge was so confused that it is impossible always to present a connected narrative. There may be discrepancies in some of the dates and many incidents have obviously been overlooked, but it is hoped that this may form a reasonably accurate guide to the events of those dark days.

More comprehensive information available from individual Battery War Diaries will weave a richer pattern upon the framework provided in the present history. Where individuals are mentioned they are given the rank held at the time of the incident.

I would like to thank Batteries for the use of their diaries; and particularly the Adjutant (Capt. Peter Thomson-Glover) and his staff for their invaluable contributions. Without this co-operation the task would have been impossible in the short space of two weeks in which the record was required.

Any profit from the sale of this book will go to the H.A.C. Old Comrades' Association, thereby helping to perpetuate the spirit of sympathy and mutual help between all ranks of the Regiment.

K. E. BOLTON.

Skrbina, 12th June, 1945.

# CONTENTS

**PART ONE : Sept., 1939—Sept., 1941**
### STAND-TO
1. Mobilisation : 121 O.C.T.U. .. .. .. .. pages 3–4
2. Training to fight .. .. .. .. .. pages 5–7
3. Embarkation .. .. .. .. .. .. pages 7–8

**PART TWO : Sept., 1941—Sept., 1942**
### RETREAT
1. Voyage and Pursuit .. .. .. .. .. pages 9–14
2. Agheila—Msus—Gazala .. .. .. .. pages 14–20
3. Knightsbridge .. .. .. .. .. .. pages 20–30
4. Way Back .. .. .. .. .. .. pages 30–34

**PART THREE : Sept., 1942—May, 1943**
### ATTACK
1. Alamein .. .. .. .. .. .. pages 35–48
2. Tmimi to Mareth .. .. .. .. .. pages 48–50
3. Left Hook .. .. .. .. .. .. pages 50–54
4. End in Africa .. .. .. .. .. .. pages 54–60

**PART FOUR : May, 1943—May, 1944**
### INVASION
1. Boating .. .. .. .. .. .. pages 61–62
2. Battle of Sicily .. .. .. .. .. pages 62–65
3. Algiers Interlude .. .. .. .. .. pages 65–66

**PART FIVE : June, 1944—May, 1945**
### VICTORY
1. Gothic Line .. .. .. .. .. .. pages 67–73
2. Conquest in Italy .. .. .. .. .. pages 73–76

**APPENDIX**
Roll of Honour .. .. .. .. .. pages 77–81
Honours and Awards .. .. .. .. pages 81–82
Commands in which the Regiment has Served .. .. page 82
Command and Appointments .. .. .. .. page 83
Summary of Battle Casualties .. .. .. .. page 84

EL ALAMEIN, October, 1942.

Self-Propelled Guns of 11th (H.A.C.) Regt. R.H.A. await the order to advance.

*From a painting by L Sgt. G. E. Ball, of "E" Bty.*

# WITH THE
# 11th (H.A.C.) REGIMENT, R.H.A.
## IN WORLD WAR II.

*By*

MAJOR KENNETH BOLTON, M.C.

---

## PART ONE

### STAND TO: SEPT., 1939 — SEPT., 1941

1. MOBILISATION: 121 O.C.T.U.

2. TRAINING TO FIGHT.

3. EMBARKATION.

### 1. Mobilisation : 121 OCTU

PERSONNEL AND TRAINING were the two main problems with which the Regiment wrestled during the two years between general mobilisation and embarkation for overseas service.

The Regiment fully realised its officer producing responsibilities and in fulfilment of these obligations sent away all potential officers as vacancies were allotted at O.C.T.Us. This obviously involved a serious drain on resources, since many of them were key men—specialists, and senior N.C.Os. with long experience. Their places were not filled by men of the standard required in an R.H.A. Regiment. Many overtures made to the War Office to obtain an improvement in the reinforcements gained little reward.

Perpetual postings to O.C.T.U. and consequent reshuffling within the Batteries prevented continuity of training despite the most dogged efforts by Regimental Instructors determined to make the Regiment ready for battle.

Even before war was declared the Regiment suffered a serious loss when a number of officers, N.C.Os. and men were taken away to form the nucleus of the 12th (H.A.C.) Regiment, R.H.A., under the Territorial Army doubling scheme. In the autumn of 1939, no fewer than 100 O.Rs. of "A" and " B " Batteries also left the Regiment for 121st and other O.C.T.U.s. Records kept by Capt. A. E. C. Green show that the Regiment continued to send candidates to O.C.T.U. from September, 1939, until two days before embarkation in September, 1941 ; by which time the number exceeded 400. Scarcely a Gunner Regiment has not had an H.A.C. officer representative during this war

The origin of training for potential officers goes back to November, 1936, when some 20 O.Rs. were chosen from "A" and " B " Batteries and the City of London Yeomanry to be trained by Capt. R. W. Goodbody (Artillery and Regimental Adjutant), for certificate "A" (artillery). They sat for the examination in the following March, when all passed the written part although two or three failed the tactical examination at the 1937 August camp. In November the " B " class was started in which another 30 O.Rs. were given a course of instruction.

These two classes formed the genesis of a far more elaborate scheme for the training season 1937-38. This was a crucial period for the Regiment in another respect. Full mechanisation was introduced, with the result that much of the equipment and many accepted technical ideas were, perforce, radically revised. The first part of the training scheme was the inauguration of an " O " class, in which 25 candidates were instructed by Lieuts. Croxton and Lazenby assisted by two A.I.G.s, B.S.M.s Fraser and Wren. Lieut B. Wilson, R.H.A., was lent from 1st R.H.A., as an additional instructor during camp. Successful candidates at the examination soon obtained commissions in the various Gunner Regiments around London.

By this time the training of future officers had developed into one of the major aims, centred in the " O " Troop commanded by Major J. A. Hill, with Lieut. B. Wilson now posted to the Regiment as Chief Instructor. T.E.W.T.s were held every weekend in addition to indoor training on two nights a week. The climax to all this endeavour came in West Down Camp in May, when for the first time full equipment was available and all candidates were able to do the various officer and W. O. duties on drill orders. No fewer than 40 candidates were successful in the final examination.

Meanwhile the international situation was rapidly deteriorating with a resulting increase of training fever. Immediately after the May camp another " B " class was started and a further 120 men qualified at the July examination to attend the course planned for the next season. These training plans never functioned because, when war broke out in September, the first whispers were heard of Officer Cadet Training Units.

In those days of mobilisation when superhuman tasks were attempted and accomplished, the 121st (H.A.C.) O.C.T.U. was created almost overnight at Aldershot, under the command of Lieut.-Col. A. H. Burne, D.S.O. Lieut. Wilson was posted as Adjutant, with Major Lazenby, 2/Lieuts. Sworder and Hay as the nucleus of the teaching staff. Peter Sworder tacitly says, " On the 14th September the 120 holders of ' B ' certificates arrived from the 11th Regiment and began training for emergency commissions." The exodus continued, not only of potential gunner officers but of candidates for commissions in the other Arms and services.

## 2. Training to Fight

THROUGHOUT THE TRYING MONTHS of 1939-40, the determination to create a fighting unit was implemented despite every setback and discouragement.

The 400 candidates for commissions were not replaced with the type of reinforcement the Regiment had a right to expect. Upon his appointment to command the Regiment in the summer of 1940, Lieut.-Col. W. A. Ebbels, M.C., resolved to clear all potential officers out of the ranks so that the Regiment could settle down to training unhampered by periodic upheavals. The War Office mistakenly believed that the Regiment still retained a large number of potential officers in its ranks. This supposition led to an investigation by Col. Archer, Permanent President, Southern Command Interview Board (O.C.T.U.), who wrote a forceful vindication of the Regiment. He reported that, far from holding potential officers, the Regiment had already posted all bar six or seven suitable men to O.C.T.U., and these men were awaiting interview by a Command Board. His report was supported by an appendix showing the O.C.T.U. postings by ranks and trades, which was at once a powerful instrument of defence and of accusation.

Even further complications impeded a rational sequence of training. Orders were received in November, 1940, to raise a third Battery to convert the Regiment into the new three-battery establishment. Up to this time the 11th Regiment had consisted of " A " and " B " Batteries; while the 12th had " C " and " D " Batteries. The 11th now created " E " Battery, while the 12th raised " F " Battery. Major Gore was appointed to command " E " Battery, which was born by the process of taking 50 officers and men from the parent "A" and " B " Batteries, causing a further inevitable weakening in "A" and "B." To make up " E " Battery to full strength the Regiment had to take in another 50 reinforcements, plus 100 to make up losses from "A" and " B." In December, 1941, Major Croxton succeeded Major Gore, who was posted to the Staff College.

This was a moment when help was indeed sorely needed, and when help most signally failed to arrive. A great proportion of the intake at this time was described by the Adjutant, Capt. Green, as " not only unsuitable for training as gunners, let alone Horse Gunners, but unfit for service in any arm, save perhaps as pioneers."

At R.H.Q. a grim " wastage or unsuitable " list was opened, which grew to such strength that eventually 72 men were posted away in one batch alone. It would seem incredible but it is nevertheless true that even after the unit was ordered to mobilise for overseas service there were 50-60 men still on the wastage list. Five of the men were complete illiterates, unable to read or write, and this is one of several individual reports : " Gnr. ......, posted as a driver, but had only four weeks' driving experience. This man had actually been posted to the 11th R.H.A., two months before as a signaller and had been returned as entirely unsuitable after fair tests. Mentally dull, and will never make a driver, signaller or gunner."

This type of misdirection in effort resulted in a letter from Lieut.-Col. Ebbels to the Director of Mobilisation, which concluded with a startling paragraph : " Out of a total of 81 N.C.O.s and men posted to the Regiment to make up deficiencies between the date when the Regiment received orders to mobilise for overseas service (24th August, 1941), to the date of completion of mobilisation, 32 N.C.O.s and men had to be returned to the supplying units for reasons of unsuitability. In fact, the completion of mobilisation of the Regiment was delayed for 7 days on account of personnel difficulties."

Understanding and help was forthcoming from several sympathetic officers in the War Office. Many men were posted away on surreptitious transfers and a further large batch was left behind, posted as home details on the eve of embarkation.

The Regiment had received a large proportion of reinforcements from infantry units and consequently experienced great trouble in obtaining signallers, R.A. drivers and specialists, most of whom had to be trained from scratch.

Efforts were constantly being made to obtain good junior officers who could be welded together into strong Battery teams. To allow for the necessary Wagon Line Officer, it was desired to increase the number of officers per battery from 10 to 11, plus another officer as first line reinforcement. The War Office would not approve this suggestion although there were over 1,000 surplus gunner officers. Nevertheless, the extra officer was obtained by private enterprise, and on 18th August, 1941, regularised through Brig. C. M. Vallentin, M.C., Commander 1st Support Group, although the instruction from Division stated that it was subject to shipping space.

Through all these storms and eruptions, the Battery Commanders, Majors Adye, Sheil and Croxton, had pushed forward their training, with Nos. 1, specialists,' signallers' and gunners' courses and drill orders, as frequently as equipment, petrol and space allowed.

In common with other units, during the early months of the war, and after Dunkirk, the Regiment had been engaged on V.P. guards and defence works in and around London and in Surrey. In May, 1941, the Regiment moved from Gomshall, Surrey, to Chilton Foliat, Berks, to complete training.

The Regiment derived valuable knowledge from advice, tactical and technical information received by "A" Battery from its attachment to 1st R.H.A., in the summer of 1940. Individual training, 25-pounder anti-tank open sight shooting and exhausting night schemes, with frequent drill orders on Salisbury Plain, all culminated in a firing camp at Sennybridge in June, 1941. At this camp, Lieut. J. P. Mills as G.P.O., "C" Troop, created a regimental record by getting off the first round 1 minute 15 seconds from the order "Action," given with the gun on wheels. Morale in the Regiment rose abruptly when Brigadier Vallentin, summing up the practice camp, said that in his opinion the Regiment was battle worthy.

The 1st Armoured Division had been with the unfortunate B.E.F. in France. The Division was re-formed soon after Dunkirk and the Regiment at once assiduously co-operated in training schemes, resuming the important process of getting to know the other Regiments.

In those days the Regiment was part of 1st Support Group. The 1st Armoured Division comprised the 2nd and 22nd Armoured Brigades besides 1st Support Group, and the Regiment was therefore in a most desirable position to study and understand the peculiar problems of both cavalry and infantry. Everyone knew the day would come when Britain would take the offensive; it was inconceivable that on that day 1st Armoured Division would be overlooked, though its destination was always a matter of wild speculation. Consequently a wide variety of subjects was included in the training to fit the Regiment for any eventuality. Map reading was varied with navigation by day and by night—in the course of which one Battery was completely dispersed in the pelting midnight rain on Salisbury Plain and was not gathered together again until the next midday. Sudden alarms were raised to test mobility. No little panic was caused when the Regiment was once called out during a weekend. Solitary Orderly Officers despatched D.R.s to neighbouring towns to round up officers and men on weekend or day pass, and in the end the Regiment, complete with all its guns, left on time.

Passing through these and many other tests, the Regiment gradually built up a resilience and confidence which was indeed fortunate in view of trials in the storm of battle. Nos. 1 were as keen as they were efficient, and by summer of 1941, the Unit had been fused into a well-balanced combination with a strong regimental pride.

## 3. Embarkation

ON 30TH JULY, 1941, THE KING AND QUEEN inspected 1st Armoured Division and visited the Regiment at Chilton Lodge, Chilton Foliat, where they watched a demonstration of quick actions. This visit was regarded by many as a sign that the Division would shortly go overseas and speculations were confirmed eight days later. Brigadier Vallentin called at R.H.Q., on 8th August, 1941, to tell the Colonel that he had received orders for 1st Support Group to mobilise for service overseas. All ranks were informed on the following day. This aroused some suspicion since it seemed directly opposed to the normal rules of security and there were those who believed this might be a bluff to deceive the enemy regarding the movements of 1st Armoured Division.

Nevertheless, the Regiment immediately lost interest in making improvements in the hutted camp for the winter and began the tremendous amount of work preparatory to embarkation. Authority was given for embarkation leave, which had to be completed in four weeks.

Desert tyres were delivered; all vehicles, armoured O.P.s, tractors and guns were rigorously inspected, and a vast assortment of strange clothing, including khaki drill and topees, was received from ordnance. No reliable information was given, but the Middle East was the favourite bet for the Regiment's destination, although there were backers for the Far East, India, Iran and even Russia.

The mobilisation order was dated 24th August, 1941, and the Regiment was ordered to mobilise for service overseas in tropical climate by 00.01 hours, on 15th September, 1941. As a result of this order, the Regiment became Priority One for deliveries from ordnance, etc., and there was an extraordinary improvement in the speed of the necessary services. The scope of these services extended from modifications to armoured O.P.s, via dental treatment, vaccinations and inoculations for all ranks, to the fitting of tropical clothing and the collection by officers of all manner of articles of kit recommended by seasoned campaigners in the Middle East. Officers wearing the Divisional " rhino " sign frequently visited London for drill uniform, corduroy slacks, goggles, etc. Security was therefore at a very low ebb and about the only thing unknown to the general public was the date upon which 1st Armoured Division would sail.

Perpetual amusement was created within the Regiment by official and private parades at which the men dressed themselves in their newly acquired K.D. uniform and it was astonishing how personalities changed under the shade of the wide-brimmed topee. The strange tropical shorts, with turn-ups almost as long as the legs, engulfed many a pair of white and knobbly knees. Curious devices such as the sun compass and the terrifying mysteries of navigation appeared in daily conversation—and later in training. Lieut. J. H. McAllum returned from a course with notes on such wizardry as " the equation of time " and " permanent magnetism of vehicle fore and aft and athwartship " which did little to encourage confidence in desert navigation or reassure those terrified by the dreadful fate which had befallen the unwary who lost themselves in the desert.

A round of social parties, which included the wedding of Capt. Green at St. Martin's-in-the-Fields and, two days later, of Major Croxton, culminated with a farewell ball at Chilton Lodge.

Even now there were still changes in personnel. Major Adye commanding "A," and Major Sheil commanding " B," both left for commands, and Major J. R. E. Benson and Major J. F. Linton joined the Regiment—Major Benson to command " B " and Major Linton as 2nd i/c when Major J. McDermid returned to "A". All ranks were urged to make wills. Arrangements were also made to form a welfare service for the Regiment and Mrs. Ebbels consented to co-ordinate the services of other officers' wives to help in the many problems which would continue to arise among the families left behind by the men, particularly those with the prospect of another winter under renewed bombing attacks.

On 12th September, Major-General the Duke of Gloucester—himself a member of the H.A.C.—paid a visit to wish the Regiment God-speed. The first convoy of vehicles left on 17th September, when nine armoured O.P.s went by rail to Birkenhead. Two days later the convoy of guns and tractors followed, also to Birkenhead ; and on successive days other vehicles went to Newport, Hull and Dumfries.

The Regimental baggage party left Chilton on 22nd September, 1941. The main body was divided into two groups, the first of 19 officers and 302 O.R.s who, laden as heavily as pack mules, marched from Chilton Lodge to Hungerford Station. The remainder left the station at midnight on 24th September. Both trains appeared to make a preliminary tour of England, eventually reaching Aintree Station via Sheffield. Buses conveyed the detachments to the docks and the Regiment embarked on board H.M.T. "Samaria."

★ ★ ★

# PART TWO

## RETREAT: SEPTEMBER, 1941—SEPTEMBER, 1942

1. VOYAGE AND PURSUIT.
2. AGHEILA — MSUS — GAZALA.
3. KNIGHTSBRIDGE.
4. WAY BACK.

## 1. Voyage and Pursuit

EMBARKATION WAS COMPLETED by the 26th September and H.M.T. "Samaria" rode in the Mersey Channel for a week before beginning the voyage. An amusing incident happened as the ship slipped away from the dockside. Capt. Bourne had been sent ashore on a Regimental detail. Crowds lining the rails as the ship slowly pulled away saw a harassed officer leap from a car which had just stopped on the hard. He raced to the water's edge—too late, for the gangway has been hauled up. There stood the dismayed Capt. Bourne watching the ship (as he confessed later), believing she was setting out for the real voyage. He was determined not to be left behind and hustling into the dock offices, ordered a tender in which he was taken aboard.

The "Samaria" left the Mersey and headed north along the Irish coast with the convoy transporting the 2nd Armoured Brigade and 1st Support Group, escorted by destroyers, an aircraft carrier and later, the cruiser H.M.S. "Devonshire." Boat drills and practices for air raid stations had been held even during the confusion of allocating berths, stowing baggage and settling down to the unaccustomed life aboard ship. They had been regarded as rather tiresome, but opinion changed within a couple of days after a German reconnaissance plane had spotted the convoy. Air raid alarms were rung in earnest and everybody prepared for a full-scale bombing attack. By extraordinary good fortune the convoy was enveloped in the security of impenetrable fog within the hour. There were no further air raid alarms throughout the voyage; although there were occasional submarine scares no offensive action was encountered.

The course zigzagged so far into the Atlantic that it was credibly reported the convoy would touch New York before sailing south down the American coast. The first two days were bitterly cold. Most of the troops were seasick, thereby at least getting that unpleasantness over early. As the convoy turned south the weather improved and the motion of the ship became steadier, so that deck sports, lectures and training—eternal training—were soon organised. Individual training in gunner subjects was varied with diversions such as semaphore; months later figures were often seen standing on the top of vehicles tic-tacking messages to each other across several thousand yards of desert.

Food was variable. As the heat increased many of the troop decks became oppressively hot. Later in the voyage almost everybody slept on deck in the open. When the "Samaria" entered the tropics milky white English complexions turned to lobster, then swarthy brown. The Regiment was being educated in the hard way to endure tropical heat. Everyone passed through the stage of suffering from heat blisters and " gyppy tummy." Gradually a better standard of smartness was attained in the issue K.D. uniforms and after a time it was possible to identify nearly everybody under the disguise of a topee.

**Officers of the 11th on board H.M.T. "Samaria," November, 1942.**

Back :—Lieut. J. H. McAllum†.
Front :—2/Lieut. M. V. Boys† ; 2 'Lieut. B. H. S. Laskey† ; Lieut. J. W. Venning† ; Capt. J. W. Hopkins, M.C.† ; Major J. R. E. Benson ; Capt. J. P. Sworder ; Lieut. G. C. de Boinville.
† Since killed or died of wounds.

Fresh water was soon rationed although it was always possible to obtain sea water baths. Early in October, the convoy put into Freetown, where nobody was allowed ashore. Bumboats bobbed around the ship from dawn to nightfall ; and the strange antics of the itinerant black men begging, diving for money, unsuccessfully trying to sell fruit, formed an inexhaustible fund of entertainment when time otherwise hung heavily in the torrid heat.

There was, it seemed, some misunderstanding about taking on fresh water. When the ship left Freetown water was even more stringently rationed. However, this was said to be good training for the parched life one would be compelled to live if the Regiment went to fight in the Western Desert. There was no reliable indication even now of the Regiment's destination and it is odd that none of the men and few of the officers knew the Regiment was bound for the desert until the "Samaria" sailed up the Red Sea to Port Tewfik.

All ranks became impatient during the long voyage of ten weeks broken only by three calls where troops were allowed ashore. The heartache of leaving home, lack of mail, and the trials of the unaccustomed life in oppressive heat, created mental and physical strain. The three places where the Regiment was allowed to go ashore were Durban, Aden and Port Sudan. Everybody received the magnificent welcome for which Durban is renowned. Residents met the troops leaving the ship, took them on sightseeing tours in cars and gave them splendid meals in their fine, cool villas. Friendships formed in Durban have lasted throughout the war. Just before entering Aden, the Regiment paraded to salute and wish good-bye to H.M.S. "Repulse," which had accompanied the convoy from Capetown. The "Repulse" steamed through the convoy, a magnificent show of grace and strength. The Regiment heard with particular sorrow the news that, after leaving the convoy, the battle-cruiser had been sunk in Far Eastern waters.

At Aden everyone visited the war memorial, to members of the H.A.C. killed in the Great War, which has been erected on the dockside.

During the voyage " E " Battery celebrated its first birthday. Other diverting incidents which helped to relieve the monotony were the ceremony of crossing the line (and consequent horseplay), concert parties, boxing tournament and the unceasing effort to outwit racketeers. Phosphorescent sparks glittered in the sea during the quiet hours of the velvet night. Star gazing became a general craze as attempts were made to master the wizardry of navigation. The chief exponent was the Regiment Survey Officer, Lieut. Trapnell, and incidentally he kept a day-to-day log of the ship's movements.

With deep relief the Regiment disembarked at Port Tewfik on 6th December. A wistful conversation overheard between two Gunners, looking over the rails at the Arabian coastline, aptly summarises the general spirit :

Said one : " Look at the mountains—just like the cliffs of Dover."

" Don't be silly, they're the wrong colour. The cliffs of Dover are as white as chalk."

" Yes, but these are like me, browned off."

At any rate the Regiment was spared the undermining influence of sailing by drafts—for the men had with them officers and N.C.O.s they knew, who were thus able to accomplish good work in maintaining morale.

After waiting some hours on Port Tewfik railway station the Regiment travelled by train to Amyria, heading for the desert with a vengeance. It was a great shock to find not a baking hot stretch of sand but icy winds whipping up a fog of brown grit which percolated everywhere, stinging, choking.

The Batteries were deposited with hand baggage and a few pieces of canvas to fend for themselves in this disagreeable sandstorm. One man had objected to going ashore in battledress—when he heard this order in the heat of the Red Sea—and he had been allowed to retain his khaki drill. He learnt one of the biggest lessons of his life.

With only a week at Amyria, everybody managed to get into Alexandria and also put in a tremendous amount of hard work sorting out vehicles, making desert modifications and calibrating guns. Vehicles over which so much trouble had been taken in U.K., were not now available and other ones were drawn from Tel-el-Kebir.

Various visiting officers lectured on desert warfare and talked about leaguering, corduroys, brewing-up and sun compasses. But it was a relief to discover that the higher arts of navigation were not really necessary in the desert, where rough and ready methods seemed to achieve desired results. Curiously enough, once the Regiment had got over its shyness and gained confidence no one was ever really lost throughout the desert campaigns; even although directions were usually—"straight on until you find a burnt-out Blenheim, then about 12 miles on about 45 degrees, and you come to Bir so-and-so—Well, you can't miss 'em then."

Contact was made with the three Regiments of 2nd Armoured Brigade with whom the Regiment was ordered to leave in pursuit of the battle, "A" Battery affiliated to The Queen's Bays, "B" Battery to the 10th Hussars, and "E" Battery to the 9th Lancers. That was how it was laid down in the beginning and that was how it remained through long and arduous battles.

On December 12th the Regiment wheeled out of camp and drove through the rain to Mersa Matruh, a distance of 180 miles. Batteries joined their own armoured Regiments, raced forward day after day across the desert to catch up with the offensive which had progressed to Benghazi.

**Major J. McDermid, H.A.C., and Major R. S. Berry, Transvaal Horse Artillery, December, 1941.**

There were occasional day halts for maintenance, but training was combined with the approach march and the usual drill was: Break leaguer at first light, brew-up, drive all morning, brew at midday, drive in the afternoon, brew again for the big meal of the day at about 17.00 hours, all fires out at sundown, close leaguer for the night with "bivvies" to be pitched, water, petrol and rations to be issued. Rations were scarce, the basic issue one tin of bully and one packet of biscuits per man, per day, supplemented occasionally by a little jam, very occasionally by bacon, seldom by vegetables. All meals were prepared on a vehicle basis. Since there is no greater incentive than eating meals of one's own cooking, everybody soon acquired a tolerable proficiency. Indeed, a lively imagination was shown in the combination of bully beef and biscuits, in disguising biscuits as "biscuit bergoo" (porridge), as jam waffles (soaked in water then fried), even as the basis of chocolates (using the tinned emergency rations), and in recipes for serving bully beef fried, boiled, stewed.

Every vehicle acquired its own set of cooking utensils, its patent oven and sooted brew can, conventionally hooked under the tailboard. Fuel for brew fires was generally petrol poured into sand, sometimes camel thorn. People at home would have been aghast at this wanton use of petrol until they realised that water was far more precious than petrol in the desert. Water was rationed at half a gallon per man per day for all purposes including radiator, so it was quite common to wash, shave, clean one's teeth complete on half a mug and that water was then used in the radiator—sometimes even strained through sand or cloth for a second use. Each vehicle carried a reserve of 3 days' water, rations and 200 miles' worth of petrol in case of misfortune.

There is no doubt the Regiment was very green in making itself comfortable. Supplies were short and there had been no time to obtain private stocks in the Delta. Consequently this was a hard, thirsty and very hungry ten weeks, during which bread was never once seen.

When Benghazi was taken, Batteries were able to get supplementary rations by purchases of tinned food, Italian stocks left behind by the retreating enemy, and—oh joy—red wine. Regular weekly N.A.A.F.I. issues of cigarettes, chocolate, etc., had not yet been instituted. There was in theory a weekly issue of 50 cigarettes per man, but for nearly six weeks there was scarcely a cigarette to be found throughout the Regiment and men often smoked dried tealeaves rolled up in message forms. After so long without a cigarette even " Vs " were treasured when supplies did come through. This may seem a dismal catalogue, yet in reality the spirits of the Regiment soared and morale had never been stronger because everybody was imbued with a driving keenness to join the battle and a fine pride, not only in the Regiment but in the whole Brigade which, as a Brigade, was fast developing its peculiar character, whimsical but aggressive.

The exhilaration of movement contributed very largely to the general high spirits. Not even the most unimaginative could be unmoved by the gallant display of an armoured Regiment in full cry—its screen of carriers, three squadrons deployed, one out in front in line astern, the other two line ahead on the flanks, guns in the middle, infantry and anti-tank guns in the rear. Careering over the desert at a cruising speed of 20 miles an hour, the tanks were for all the world like a battle squadron of warships spread out to the far horizon. In this way the Regiment reached the wire marking the frontier between Egypt and Libya. There the sound of gunfire was heard for the first time as 30 Corps' troops beseiged the German and Italian garrison in Halfaya Pass.

The Regiment reached the wire in a blinding sandstorm in which many small parties became scattered and lost until next day, when everybody rejoined in the area of Bir el Gibni, having crossed the wire at either Bir Shefersen or Sidi Omar. Ist R.H.A., and other troops who had withstood the seige of Tobruk came down the Trigh Capuzzo on their way back to rest. Several parties from the Batteries drove into Tobruk to stare in bewilderment at the desolation so surprising since, from a distance, the town looked undamaged and very attractive. Everyone was impressed, too, with the simple dignity of the memorial erected by the Australians to those who had fallen in Tobruk. After a few days near Bir Harmat the Regiment moved forward again, Batteries with Regimental groups, on to Tengeder, Msus and Antelat.

The offensive launched by General Auchinleck had passed beyond Benghazi to Agedabia, while the Afrika Korps had retreated to Agheila, holding a line some 12 miles from the coast to the impassable Wadi Faregh and the salt lakes. During the long march, and particularly towards its end, there were many signs of battle and relics of the Afrika Korps equipment were curiously inspected by troops who were still intrigued by the Palm and Swastika sign painted on vehicles and guns.

The speed of the advance outran supplies. Therefore, until supplies could be built up for another offensive, it was decided to harass the enemy with " Jock columns." Orders were received that the Batteries would be allocated to three columns—"A" to Baron column—"B" to James column—and "E" to Charles column, so named after their commanders, Lieut.-Col. (Baron) Ebbels, Lieut.-Col. James Bosville and Lieut.-Col. Charles Sismey. The Regiment was disappointed about leaving the armoured Regiments, for Batteries had by this time grown familiar with their methods and made strong friendships. It was felt wiser to enter battle for the first time in an accustomed order, with the various drills practised and learnt during the approach march. However, the orders were obeyed with alacrity since there was the invigorating prospect of a real fight against the Germans after so much preparation, yearning and, finally, sheer racing to overtake the battlefront.

Seasoned desert rats explained that "Jock columns" were really rather good fun. With this further encouragement, the Batteries set out after Christmas in a spirit of gay adventure. When the 2nd R.H.A. were encountered, on their way back for a rest, they gave an ominous warning that the going, especially in the Wadi Faregh, was extremely treacherous and the soft, deep sand was really "not on" for quick movement. A few days later, the Regiment wholeheartedly agreed. On the way down towards Agheila the new Divisional Commander, General Frank Messervy, met officers and wished the columns success. Everybody believed a "Jock column" was rather like practice camp with extra zest, because shells would be directed on the enemy. Whenever threatened with a serious engagement, the drill was clear—simply "limber up, drive away and pop up somewhere else." There was also a general belief from intelligence sources that the entire German tank force did not exceed 15. None of the impressions proved accurate.

The Batteries began to wonder whether this particular expanse of desert was suitable for movement of any sort, never mind the tip and run warfare which the "Jock columns" involved. Quite commonly a gun would be winched for a full hour to move half a mile. Many stories have been told of the days that followed the "Msus Stakes." No one who saw the unflagging work both day and night, the tenacity and bravery in action by sleepless men who had inadequate rations and less water, can doubt that these were in fact, among the finest achievements of the whole Regimental history. It is difficult to state exactly how many guns were left in the Regiment at any one time, because replacements were constantly being picked up from other units and occasionally one or other of the Regiment's guns would be lost, to rejoin in another position, but at Charruba, which may be regarded as the end of the "Jock column" debacle, the Regiment had 11 guns. The others had been knocked out in actions over open sights or abandoned, utterly bogged and destroyed.

## 2. Agheila—Msus—Gazala

"A" BATTERY, COMMANDED BY MAJOR MCDERMID, set out with "Baron" column towards the Agheila line, negotiating difficult sand dunes to close into the German defended localities, and fired the first rounds on 18th January, 1942. Three days later a heavy barrage fell as the Battery was again preparing to harass the enemy in the early morning, and approximately 90 Mark III tanks appeared in a semi-circle 4,000 yards away, leading what was later described as a "reconnaissance in force." The Battery was forced to withdraw about 20 miles through almost impassable sand dunes, stopping to occupy some seven positions for rearguard actions in which O.P.s began targets and the range closed into open sights, with artillery and machine-gun fire sweeping the guns.

Perpetual low gear work overheated engines. Radiators were blown, other trucks became hopelessly bogged and were hit. Near the Bettafal bottleneck 18 Stukas dive-bombed the column to destroy more equipment. Two guns had already been lost, but F Sub. went into action and fought over open sights under machine-gun fire from armoured cars until, hopelessly bogged, this gun was abandoned. In the very first position one " D " Troop gun and tractor were hit and the crew brought back on RD. Two more " D " Troop guns were abandoned when they were bogged under heavy machine-gun fire. The Battery, therefore, had only two guns—B and H Subs.—after negotiating the bottleneck.

During the night the column moved 10 miles further east and carried on along the Antelat track the next day. On the afternoon of 23rd January, the two guns were ordered into action on a ridge near Saunnu, where a number of British tanks were withdrawing. A troop of South African 25-pounders on the left were also sited in an anti-tank rôle. The C.O. directed fire standing on the gun position. Later Major Benson, the 2nd i/c arrived to join Capt. Dunn and Lieuts. Mills, Armitage, Hart and Drage. The two Nos. 1 were Sgt. Wraight and Sgt. Town. Thirteen enemy tanks appeared and as the range closed the guns were ordered to engage. Each gun fired about half-a-dozen rounds and both were then hit almost simultaneously. Lieut. Mills, who was laying on B Sub., was seriously wounded and two other members of the sub. were also casualties. The tanks closed in supporting each other with fire and movement, and swept the position with intense machine-gun fire. Sgt. Town was killed and most of his detachment killed or wounded ; Lieut. Armitage took Sgt. Town's place, but was killed serving the gun. Finally, the crews were ordered to leave their smashed guns and get out as best they could. B Sub. squad carried 10 men.

Meanwhile, Capt. Gilbert and Lieut. Hart had joined the South African guns, rallying some of the crews, and during the ensuing action Lieut. Hart received wounds from which he died.

Major Benson and Lieut. Drage continued to fight the single remaining gun, which was hit several times and the sights completely shot away. They aimed by squinting along the piece. Both were wounded in the leg. When they attempted to escape in a truck it was set on fire by a tank. They jumped out under machine-gun fire and feigned death. German tanks closed on to the position. One passed within three yards of the two figures sprawling in the sand, but the tank commander was satisfied that they were dead and did not stop. Major Benson and Lieut. Drage stayed there until darkness when they began a two-day trek, in the course of which they disguised themselves as Bedouins, until ultimately they were picked up by a Rifle Brigade carrier and returned to the Regiment.

Lieut. Buchanan had stayed behind to help repair a vehicle. His party was surprised and captured by a German armoured-car patrol. After picking up valuable information from the German leaguer in which he spent the night, Lieut. Buchanan escaped next day and rejoined safely. He was under escort back when the Dodge truck stopped to help unditch a German vehicle. He and his guards dismounted—while the Germans were heaving around the bogged vehicle, Lieut. Buchanan jumped into the Dodge and drove away. The vibration of the truck set off a machine gun mounted in the back and the Germans must have been very shaken by the mad Englishman who both drove and fired backwards at the same time.

"A" Battery were ordered back to Charruba and Mechili, then to Tobruk where they were given 200 Italian prisoners and 1 German officer to escort. The German officer was very obstreperous, would not travel with the Italians and was eventually tied down and guarded by four armed men. Early in February the Battery arrived at Smugglers' Cove, near Mersa Matruh, to refit and reform.

"B" Battery had been engaged in a similar running fight on the southern flank. After driving south down the Antelat track and negotiating the escarpment at Bettafal, "James" column had reached its base on 19th January. Guns were winched over half the way and some of the vehicles, stuck in the soft shifting sand, were left behind to come on as soon as possible. All rejoined except the "Q" truck and a quad sent back to tow it out from the sand dunes near Bettafal. These were cut off and captured when the enemy appeared without warning on 21st January. Lieut. Waugh, who was in charge of the party, Sgt. Lacey the Fitter Sgt. and B.Q.M.S. Murray were among those who were captured.

"James" column leaguered some 10 miles from the German positions. The German line ran in front of "A" Battery, along the coastal belt to the edge of a steep east-west escarpment which fell sheer to a wide sandy basin, treacherous and flat except for two or three rocky outcrops called "The Pimples" about five miles west of the leaguer. On the left of the depression dried salt lakes had not been traversed either by ancient caravan or modern carrier. A Rifle Brigade patrol in Bren carriers was dispatched south to come in near Marada behind the German positions. This patrol was well inside the German lines when the counter-attack started, was lost and believed captured for several days until the carriers suddenly turned up once more near Saunnu. On their way, by the most extraordinary coincidence and good fortune, they met and picked up two solitary "wogs" walking across the desert who turned out to be Major Benson and Lieut. Drage.

On 20th January, the Battery occupied gun positions and O.Ps. were sent forward with escorts of carrier-borne infantry and anti-tank portees to occupy "The Pimples." Here they saw action for the first time when one of the escorts was strafed by enemy aeroplanes. Reconnaissance planes had flown over the column the previous day and here was confirmation that the Germans knew of its presence. The next day even stronger proof was forthcoming.

Early on the morning of 21st January, Major Linton left with other officers to reconnoitre a possible route forward through the sand dunes so that a section of guns might be taken out during darkness to occupy positions from which they could fire. The targets were to be whatever the Pimple O.P. might see on the tableland which surmounted the blank wall of rock five miles away across the sand basin. As a matter of fact the only enemy seen on 20th January, was an armoured car patrol, which appeared on top of the escarpment, and two Germans dismounted for five minutes before driving off again. During the morning of 21st January, the rumble of gunfire was heard from the north. Everybody in the Battery leaguer was engaged on maintenance when, without warning, the order "action" was given over the Battery net. Petrol tanks were almost empty, so several of the guns and limbers were ferried to the troop positions by quads that happened to have rather more petrol than the others.

The guns were sited behind a low ridge on the north-west perimeter of the leaguer. "F" Troop fired the first round at 12,000 yards. In the distance a dark mass of vehicles, shimmering in the heat haze, moved slowly along the escarpment raising a tremendous cloud of dust. Capt.

Hopkins, who was doing O.P., continued to range with ever decreasing ranges until he ordered " Gun control—open sights."

The enemy column pressed forward inexorably; first tanks, then guns, then troop carriers with their echelons. The guns were now firing over open sights into a mass of vehicles. Several direct hits were scored. The wireless intercept at Corps that night picked up many lamentations from Germans whose supply echelons had been severely mauled in this action.

The Germans advanced steadily, working forward with their mobile anti-tank guns, armoured-cars and tanks until the range had dropped to 1,200 yards. About this time, the reconnaissance party returned and Major Linton gave orders to withdraw 20 miles to another leaguer. Echelons moved back first. The guns continued to fire until all the ammunition on the positions had been expended. Covering each other out, they were all safely withdrawn through heavy counter-battery fire which was brought down by German guns. The last gun out fired five parting shots at a mobile anti-tank gun trying to sneak round the left flank.

Late in the afternoon the Battery was rounded up and the guns sited in an anti-tank rôle round the perimeter of the leaguer. At this crucial moment petrol supplies miraculously arrived. The guns were pulling out of action when a wave of enemy aeroplanes came over to dive-bomb the unprepared column. No one had even a scratch for a slit trench, but 35 minutes later, when the planes flew away, nearly everybody had succeeded in burying himself in the sand, using bare hands and steel helmets.

Stukas first dive-bombed the column and the Bofors A.-A. guns which immediately opened up were silenced by the first wave. After all bombs had been dropped the Stukas and escorting fighters, among them even CR.42s, flew round and round the leaguer, machine-gunning from 20 feet. Several lorries, including the petrol lorry, were destroyed, others damaged, but not a soul in the Battery was injured although there were casualties among other units in the column, especially the A.-A. gunners who had shown great bravery. The depleted column moved forward a mile or so to form close leaguer as dusk fell. " E " Troop had four guns, " F " Troop ferried 3 guns into leaguer with two quads left after burst radiators and damage in the air raid, H Sub missed the route in the darkness and drove past; this gun was eventually lost in the sand-bog, though the crew turned up safely a week later.

" F " Troop fitters' three-tonner, with B.S.M. Kay, had been damaged by machine-gun fire. S/Sgt. Goodman and Bdr. Davies set to work mending holes in the radiator. The crew took turns on guard in the darkness as the Germans closed round the position. German voices were heard discussing the knocked-out vehicles. At midnight the fitters thought their work complete, only to find that when the engine was started the radiator was completely beyond repair. They then walked over to another truck near a blazing petrol lorry, calmly removed the radiator which they substituted for their own. They then started up and reached leaguer just in time to move with the Battery in the small hours.

No one in the column had been able to get any sleep. From noises off it was clear that the Germans were surrounding the position. At about 04.00 hours, the column moved north, starting off in close formation. All the guns got away except G Sub which had no tractor. First a fifteen-hundredweight, then the newly arrived fitters' three-tonner, then both together, with gunners straining at the gun-wheels, tried to move the gun but it was hopelessly bogged. The only result of a solid hour's work was that by now the vehicles were bogged. These were eventually dug out, the gun was smashed and the rear party moved off. This party caught up column headquarters leaguered for a breakfast brew. Other vehicles and guns were lost in the darkness but it was hoped they would rejoin later, as in fact they all did. Determined to round them up, Major Linton drove back in an eight-hundredweight to the previous night's leaguer and unhappily was there taken prisoner by the Germans in occupation.

"James" column was then ordered back towards Saunnu. Divisional Headquarters had apparently believed that the column must be captured or destroyed. German forces had broken through and in the next few days there were continual engagements as elements met, exchanged shots and veered away again. Capt. Sworder, lost in his Bren carrier, made a ground station of his wireless set, ranged the wavebands until he picked up "A" Battery's net. The operator was suspicious but Major McDermid recognised Capt. Sworder's voice at "strength one" and was able to give directional help. When Capt. Sworder eventually rejoined the Battery he brought along a spare 25-pounder gun from a column he had helped to organise out of a heterogeneous collection of lost souls.

Several times during the ensuing days "James" column was surrounded, once drove in and out of a German leaguer by night and was later saved only by fog which cloaked the escape at "Well with Windpump," near Antelat. Guns were leapfrogged by sections to cover the withdrawal against enemy armoured-cars and tanks.

Beyond Saunnu the column drove along the edge of the salt lake and that night, meeting "E" Battery and elements of 1st Support Group, formed up for a final desperate attempt to escape. The Germans closed in all round. Petrol tanks were almost dry. A raiding party sent out to a known dump returned with a certain amount of petrol plus an astonished German sentry. Nevertheless, no one had sufficient petrol and it was decided to drain some tanks to fill others until everybody could make 50 miles. All the men were loaded on the few remaining vehicles; equipment and vehicles left behind were burnt. Men swarming on the outside of quads and fifteen-hundredweights were all armed to the teeth, a desperate collection of brigands. Enemy flares closed in an ominous circle. If the exercise finished on foot it was resolved to make for the Djebel where perhaps one could live on the land.

However, it is probable that the Germans were far more scared than the escaping column. Led by Brigadier Vallentin and Headquarters 1st Support Group, the force broke through the enemy without mishap. The column drove 25 miles, halted a few minutes, then drove forward again in a pall of choking dust across rough country until drivers were almost exhausted by the strain.

At dawn the column stopped for a rest and those who had the materials managed to get breakfast and a brew of tea. Someone found a petrol dump and the vehicles managed to reach the green valley of Charruba, where the guns were put into action again. To the unbounded joy of the parched gunners, they found a stream behind the position—clear water, except for tiny red insects, but quite the best obtained since the Delta. All water cans were filled and months later an especially good brew would be explained by the remark "Charruba water"—which had become a byword in the Regiment. Capt. Hopkins had commanded the Battery through these adventures and it was largely through his guidance that so much had been retrieved and so many men extricated from the disastrous engagements. The Battery then had six guns left and a few days later a joint "B/E" Battery was formed. Surplus personnel left on loan to 2nd R.H.A.

"E" Battery had concentrated near El Agheila, where two minor dive-bombing attacks fortunately inflicted no casualties, and, on the night of 20th January, the Battery joined 2nd K.R.R.C. to form "Charles" column. Gunfire was heard from the west next morning and the Battery was ordered to move five miles on a bearing of 270 degrees, then go into action. The role of the column was to protect supply echelons. One round was fired from this position and orders received to withdraw seven miles on 90 degrees. Great difficulty was experienced getting the guns across the sand dunes. The quads winched most of the time. Every hour there was a Stuka raid.

The guns went into action to engage a column of tanks from 6,000 yards down to open sights. Other enemy tanks working round the flanks gained hull down positions and shot up the guns.

Behind this position was a high ridge of sand dunes. While struggling to get over the dunes three quads and guns were hit by enemy tanks. The crews were picked up by ammunition quads. B Sub detachment repaired a deserted infantry fifteen-hundredweight and rejoined the Battery twelve hours later. Stukas bombed the leaguer that night. Lieut. Tompson died of wounds, Gnr. Hills was killed and ten others who were wounded were evacuated, but the ambulance column was captured by the enemy.

"Charles" column withdrew to El Haseit on 22nd January. There was now no doubt that this was no small scale raid by enemy tanks but a powerful armoured counter-offensive. On the 23rd the column moved north to Antelat. Enemy tanks which had by-passed up during the night fought a bloody battle with 2nd Armoured Brigade tanks in which the two guns of "A" Battery, previously mentioned, were destroyed in action. The superiority of the Mark III over Honeys and Crusaders equipped with 37 millimetre and 2-pounders resulted in a very heavy toll of 2nd Armoured Brigade tanks, despite the extraordinary bravery of their crews.

"E" Battery drove for the second night through the enemy lines and took up positions on the north escarpment of the Saunnu basin where, at first light next day, an enemy close leaguer was surprised 4,000 yards away. There was some doubt of its identity, but a subaltern in the 60th drove to within 500 yards and, when shot at, stood up waving a red flag. The Battery then engaged and, from later information, it was learnt that 200 casualties had been inflicted by shells which fell near a cookhouse. British three-tonners among the German tanks and armoured cars (several of which were destroyed) turned out to belong to "Charles" column, including the Battery "B" Echelon, which had been ambushed in a steep-sided wadi from which only two vehicles escaped by climbing the wadi wall.

On the 25th the enemy advanced again. "E" Battery fell back with enemy columns on its flank and that night leaguered with 1st Support Group Headquarters, joined in the column which broke through the surrounding enemy lines and escaped to Charruba.

The composite "B/E" Battery, commanded by Major Croxton, after two days at Charruba moved out with a large force of cruiser tanks but made no contact with the enemy. The reported 2,000 enemy vehicles turned out to be camels! The Battery moved back to the Tengeder position as part of the left flank protection to the main forces on the coast road. Capt. Pearson, with a section and "A" Company, Rifle Brigade, under command of Major Kerr, moved to Bir Zeidan.

For the first time a party was sent back to Tobruk to obtain N.A.A.F.I. goods. It returned with unbelievable delights—cigarettes, whisky, gin cordial, chocolates, besides soap, razor blades, writing paper and stamps. The effect was miraculous!

Positions were occupied near Sidi Muftah in "Happy Valley," a pleasant stretch of desert carpeted by sweet scented purple stock. The guns helped to hold the Trigh Capuzzo in this sector for the next three months.

## 3. Knightsbridge

DURING MARCH AND APRIL there was a lull in the war in the Western Desert. The Regiment occupied positions in the centre of the Gazala Line which stretched south from the South African sector on the coast, in front of the Acroma forts, across the Trigh Capuzzo, through "Happy Valley" to Bir Aslagh, to Bir Harmat and the Free French in Bir Hacheim. The whole front was protected by wire and minefields. Gradually the Batteries were re-equipped and training schemes were held, usually in the form of wild races with armoured regiments and quick drill orders.

"Fox" Troop (late "Harry"), "E" Battery Command Post.

The first allotment of training courses was received and leave was started in the Delta. The Regiment was also called upon to help in four "Jock" columns, although the "Jock" column had outworn its usefulness since originally employed against the Italians by Brigadier "Jock" Campbell. Soldiers of the Afrika Korps were too wary and too experienced to be materially worried by "Jock" columns and seldom allowed one to penetrate dangerously into their lines of communication. Nevertheless, "Jock" columns helped to keep the battle moving and at the same time prevented the enemy from closing in across the 20 miles no-man's-land to the south.

Three columns passed off with reasonable success and without any untoward incidents save the physical hardships and certain nervous strain. But early in March "H" Troop of "E" Battery were sent out with a column of Free French, with whom they concentrated near Rotunda Segnali. The column ended in tragedy, but the supreme bravery of " H " Troop earned honour unsurpassed in the long history of the Company.

The French had information of an enemy force located in the area, but no action had taken place. Then, early one morning, an urgent warning of the approach of an enemy column was received. The Troop was busy on maintenance, but in a few minutes the guns were limbered up and on the move, led by Lieut. Venning. Capt. Colley was reconnoitring an O.P. and gave orders for the Troop to move to a more favourable position.

Suddenly, as the guns were moving, there appeared about 3,000 yards away to a flank, an enemy column heading for the French Headquarters. Venning gave the alarm signal on his hunting horn and led the guns into action. Within a few minutes it was clear that the enemy force was much larger than had been expected. At least 30 tanks turned to attack the troop. While tanks engaged the guns from hull down positions in the front, others worked round the flanks and rear. Gradually they closed in, machine-gunning and shelling the guns. Capt. Colley, the Troop Commander, returned from the O.P. and ordered the G truck away. He joined Lieut. Venning with the guns.

The enemy tanks drew closer, finally charged and over-ran the guns, Lieut. Venning and eight others were killed. The tanks then pushed on, but by this time the French Headquarters had managed to escape. Capt. Colley and others went round attending to the wounded. As soon as movement was seen two German armoured cars rounded up the survivors and marched them away. Capt. Colley and eighteen others were captured, many of them wounded, and one other rank was reported missing. Lieut. Sewell, with B.S.M. Isherwood, succeeded in getting back with the troop echelon.

General Koenig, the French Commander at Bir Hacheim, wrote a very touching letter to the C.O. and recommended the award of the Croix de Guerre to the troop. He said that the action had saved the French Headquarters, that the superb bravery of the troop was typified in one sight—a gunner lying dead still holding his rifle, by his side five spent cartridges which he had shot as the enemy tanks charged. The guns, shot-up and badly damaged, were later recovered by " E " Battery. The troop was reformed in " Happy Valley," receiving reinforcements and new guns.

" A " Battery then sent out two columns. The first " Barcol," lasted ten days until the end of April. The column was commanded by Major Barclay, The Queen's Bays, and consisted of the Battery and a squadron of Honey tanks, working with The Royals and a column of Free French near Mechili. There were one or two brisk encounters with tanks, and plenty of shooting at enemy transport and working parties. The Battery was machine-gunned by aeroplanes, but had only one casualty. Some time later " B " Troop went out with The Bays " Honey " Squadron to give support to the 12th Lancers armoured car screen. They got some shooting, but there was no real engagement.

As " Barcol " was turning back towards home, " A " Battery guns passed quite close to " Welcol," a column going out under the new C.O. Lt.-Col. Ebbels, who had left on promotion to C.R.A. of the new 10th Armoured Division, then being formed, had been succeeded by Lt.-Col. Vaughan Hughes. " Welcol " was composed of " B " Battery, now cammanded by Major Sworder, a squadron of 8th Royal Tank Regiment, Valentine tanks disguised under sunshields as three-tonners, a company of 1st Rifle Brigade, anti-tank and Bofors A.-A. guns. The column was directed upon the aerodrome near Mechili. On the third day out the guns were just about to occupy fire positions, when a large force of enemy tanks was reported to be bearing down from the north. This began a tiring game of hide and seek. " Welcol " veered this way and that in the choking heat until navigation became almost impossible—in any case maps were two squares out in the whole of that area where, as it happened, the Libyan grid changed.

The enemy tanks were not allowed to catch up and the column drew down towards the Guards in the south. Meanwhile, another force of British " I " tanks set out in the north and succeeded in drawing the enemy away, albeit with serious loss in the battle which developed. " Welcol " advanced once more and at dusk one evening galloped up a section for an exciting open sight shoot against a patrol of armoured cars. The Battery settled down to a programme of harassing fire on transport and infantry, firing some thousands of rounds.

These were the preliminary encounters of the major battle which began at Knightsbridge on 27th May. Knightsbridge was the beginning of a continuous battle day and night for 52 days, in which the Regiment suffered by far its worst casualties of the whole war. Nine officers and 54 other ranks were killed ; 18 officers and 159 other ranks wounded ; 10 officers and 201 other ranks were captured, many of them also wounded. Total casualties for the whole action were 37 officers and 475 other ranks. It is quite impossible to describe the fighting, the endurance, the humour and the tragedy which these figures represent. Knightsbridge was so nearly a victory, yet turned into defeat which began that long retreat through Tobruk, Fort Capuzzo, Sollum, Mersa Matruh back to El Alamein, where, only 60 miles from Alexandria, General Auchinleck said, " So far, but no further, this is where we stand."

A week or two before Knightsbridge the Regiment had moved back to rejoin 2nd Armoured Brigade for a period of rest at Bir el Gubi, and Delta leave re-opened. The Duke of Gloucester, who was in the M.E.F. at this time, visited the Regiment and other units in the Brigade.

The Afrika Korps and the Desert Army raced to get ready for the attack, since experience had proved that the army with the initiative was bound to win in the desert, where unlimited space enabled manœuvre and bold pincer movements to isolate strongpoints and outflank defence systems.

On the British side, new Grant tanks with a 75-millimetre gun in the hull were just arriving from America, and a proportion had already been issued to 2nd Armoured Brigade to strengthen the squadrons of Honeys and cruisers. Six-pounder anti-tank guns, still on the secret list, were also being delivered for the first time. A number was given to 239th Battery which had been detached from the 76th (later 60th) Anti-Tank Regiment to become the anti-tank Battery under command of 11th H.A.C., with Major Charlton as Battery Commander. Training with the new equipment was limited and both Grant tanks and 6-pounder guns were still arriving after the battle had started.

On the other hand the Germans had improved their tanks and were now putting Mark IVs with 75-millimetre guns into the field, while they had obtained a great number of devastating 88-millimetre dual-purpose A.-A. and anti-tank gun. Bold use of the Mark IV and 88-millimetre gun decided the battle.

At the beginning of Knightsbridge the order of battle was as follows :—
General Rommel, commanding the Afrika Korps and Italians :—
15th Panzer, 21st Panzer and 90th Light Division ; Marx Force (3rd

33rd Reconnaissance Regiments); Ariete, Littorio, Brescia, Bologna, Trieste, Trento and Folgore Divisions, with the Muller Group.

Rommel had approximately 600 tanks, mostly German, and 90,000 infantry, mostly Italian.

General Ritchie, commanding the British 8th Army under General Auchinleck, Commander-in-Chief Middle East, had the following in the line :—

> 1st British Armoured and 7th British Armoured Divisions; 1st Army Tank Brigade, three Armoured Car Regiments, 1st and 2nd South African Divisions ; 50th (TT) and 5th Indian Divisions, Free French.

Ritchie had 500 tanks and 84,000 infantry.

The battle of Knighsbridge can be divided into four phases up to the fall of Tobruk.

Phase 1. 15th Panzer, 90th Light and Littorio by-pass Bir Hacheim, reach the Knightsbridge box, severely maul 7th Armoured Division. 21st Panzer and Ariete isolate Bir Hacheim. Italian infantry attack 50th Division and South African Divisions frontally, reaching the minefield. Marx Force reach El Adem but are destroyed. 1st and 7th British Armoured Divisions in the counter-attack against 15th Panzer and 90th Light press the enemy back to the minefield. 1st South African and 50th Division hold the Italian infantry. 5th Indian Division concentrate at Bir Harmat.

Phase 2. 15th Panzer, 90th Light and Littorio, with a bridgehead on the Trigh Capuzzo minefield gap, face 1st Armoured Divison and try to work round north of Eluet el Tamar, then attempt to attack the Knightsbridge box frontally. The minefield gap is expanded for the main attack. 21st Panzer and Ariete continue the attack on Bir Hachiem, while the Italian infantry contain 1st South African and 50th Divisions. 1st Armoured Division batters the German armour in an attempt to reduce the Trigh Capuzzo bridgehead and also blocks the northern gap near Eluet el Tamar. 1st Army Tank Brigade cover Tamar. 5th Indian Division is brought up to help 1st Armoured Division by attacking the bridgehead, while 1st South African and 50th Divisions repel Italians.

Phase 3. 15th Panzer and Littorio press north behind 50th Division and attack along Trigh Capuzzo from the west. 90th Light attack and over-run 5th Indian Division. 21st Panzer and Littorio capture Bir Hacheim and press on to El Adem, turning to attack the southern flank of 2nd Armoured Brigade and over-run the remaining independent boxes south of Trigh Capuzzo. 1st British Armoured Division moves to Naduret el Ghescuasc to counter enemy armour. 1st Army Tank Brigade attempts to guard the exposed flank of 50th Division. 1st South African Division withdraw towards Tobruk. 50th Division counter-attacks the Italian infantry and breaks out. Remnants of 5th Indian Division fall back to complete the line facing south between Knightsbridge and 1st Armoured Division.

Phase 4. German forces effect junction on the Trigh Capuzzo, cutting off all remaining troops south of that line and then press north—on the left towards Acroma on the right towards El Adem—to squeeze out Tobruk. Meanwhile flying columns cross the wire at Sidi Omar, outflanking the British defence of Sollum. On 20th June, the main assault is mounted on Tobruk from the south-east. 1st Armoured Division withdraw to the line of the escarpment. Guards Brigade evacuate Knightsbridge box by night. Whole force is ordered to Sollum to occupy defences along the escarpment of Halfaya. 1st South African Division leave their Divisional artillery and one infantry brigade to strengthen Tobruk defences and remainder are ordered to Sollum. 50th Division withdraw to Sollum. 5th Indian Division join Tobruk garrison.

After Tobruk the main German forces turned east and drove on by successive bounds towards the Delta.

Knightsbridge was a peculiarly unhappy battle. No one ever seemed to know exactly what was happening, why the Batteries had been ordered here or there, where flanking formations had reached, or indeed to have any reliable information about what was happening.

Normal regimental activity continued on May 26th. At breakfast next morning orders were received to concentrate with 2nd Armoured Brigade near Bir Lifa. Each Battery drew up inside its regimental box in the usual desert formation. The Brigade turned south and by 11.00 hours were engaging an enemy column on its way north. Thus attacked, the enemy sheered off to the west. The Brigade also wheeled to engage the column in a running fight. The Bays, then 9th Lancers, attacked, with the Regiment continually in action firing troop targets in support. Many German tanks were knocked out, transport destroyed and guns overrun. The battle had opened so suddenly that the Lieut.-Quartermaster with another officer going on a course were captured as they drove unconcernedly towards Capuzzo.

The next day the battle continued in much the same way, with 2nd Armoured Brigade moving westwards and the situation seemed well in hand. The Batteries were in action near the cross tracks marked by a huge signpost labelled "Knightsbridge," where the Guards, with 2nd R.H.A., had established a box to form the pivot of the defence. 10th Hussars with "B" Battery were immediately in front of the box, with 9th Lancers and "E" Battery at Bir Aslagh and The Bays on the other flank with "A" Battery.

The Germans retaliated with strong armoured attacks. Although all three Regiments participated in the defence, the main burden fell initially upon 10th Hussars. The 10th charged an anti-tank gun position with 2nd "B" Battery O.Ps. controlling fire on to the objective, which was successfully overrun. Other anti-tank guns were knocked out and 500 prisoners taken. The 10th Hussars, who had fought magnificently, were so severely mauled that the Regiment had to be withdrawn after a few days.

All three Batteries came under heavy counter-battery and machine-gun fire. All did their share of open sight shooting at tanks, besides indirect fire in opportunity shoots and fire plans. Casualties were numerous from shellfire, machine-gun fire and bombing, but the troops dug in stubbornly and gave no ground.

Several of the Regiment's guns received direct hits. Crews, reduced by severe casualties, kept the guns in action, while gun fitters performed astonishing tasks, both in bravery and in technical skill, to keep the guns serviceable. After three or four days of this type of fighting the Germans lost the initiative and began to retire through a gap in the minefield. Everybody was in great heart. It was believed the Afrika Korps had been thrown back with such heavy losses that a further attack would not be feasible. The enemy continued to hold the ridge west of Aslagh despite several tank attacks, including one under a mile-wide smoke screen which was fired twice by the Regiment.

It was then that 5th Indian Division were brought up to attack the Bir Aslagh position. 9th Lancers were withdrawn to refit and "B" and "E" Batteries fought mainly in support of 1st Rifle Brigade, moving north-west to the area of Bir Tamar. The Bays still had fighting squadrons left with "A" Battery in direct support.

The battle remained static for some days, while the enemy armour sat in hull-down positions from which it was impossible to dislodge them. One evening the Regiment's O.P.s were each told to engage two tanks, with single guns, as destructive targets using 100 rounds per gun. Some months later, when this area was revisited, it was interesting to observe how accurately the rounds had fallen and pleasing to find so many tanks, including Mark IIIs. and the Italian M.13, abandoned with tracks damaged by shellfire.

By 2nd June, both Major Sworder and Major Croxton, commanding " B " and " E " respectively, had been wounded. Their places were taken by Capt. Hopkins and Capt. Maclaren. Major Charlton was killed on the position manning a 6-pounder anti-tank gun.

Batteries then began to wheel round and round the Knightsbridge box in support of one attack after another or to thicken up defence. Throughout the whole of this period the guns were firing at an average range of about 3,000 yards. The gun positions received hot counter-battery fire and were raided by Stukas, but in spite of the heavy casualties and the mental strain morale was still tremendous, with a remarkable spirit of cheerful endurance among all ranks.

5th Indian Division made their attack at Bir Aslagh and on 2nd June it was clear that the Division was in difficulties. The Brigade group then wheeled to a position near Bir Harmát in order to protect the south flank. A large amount of German transport which had run on to the minefield was destroyed, but before the German column approaching from the south had been engaged the Regiment was ordered to move into the gun area of 5th Indian Division. This was in the basin where four regiments had already deployed their 96 25-pounders, and it was virtually impossible to find any space for another gun position. Tanks sat on three sides engaged in heavy fighting with the advancing German armour, while enemy gunners poured shells into the basin.

Just before dusk the German column moving up from the south was reported close at hand. The armour was slow moving round and enemy tanks penetrated the Indian echelon before they could be counter-attacked.

While the Aslagh basin was under intense fire, with machine gun bullets whistling in from two sides through the fog of smoke, orders were received to move out and go back to support the Guards in the Knightsbridge box. The Regiment formed up in close column. Almost every gun and vehicle had incredible escapes from shellfire. During the night the Regiment moved out of the doomed Aslagh basin. The Germans surrounded the force there, poured down fire from the commanding rim, and finally overran all 96 guns—indeed, only a small proportion of the gunners escaped on foot.

While the Batteries were moving in groups, with O.P.s out in the customary formation, the guns ran into an ambush near Bir Lifa. A German column which had apparently circled round in the darkness, brought four 88-millimetres into action on the crest of the ridge covering the wide, shallow wadi behind the Guards box. " B " and " E " Batteries stopped in their tracks and went into action over open sights with an average range of 1,600 yards. The guns were then fired both over open sights with gun control and as troops by the O.P. officers, who kept their Honey tanks moving.

A Sub of " E " Battery received a direct hit which killed two men, including Sgt. Swingler, the No. 1. Lieut. M. V. Boys was badly wounded and died later in the hospital ship. " H " Troop had one of their guns hit, with the complete crew wounded ; the other three guns stood firm and shot as a troop. Bdr. Kirk showed fine leadership, organising the evacuation of casualties. Major Victor Turner, who was in command of the battalion of Rifle Brigade with the Battery, and Lieut. McAllum, brought up ammunition under intense fire. All of the 88's were knocked out.

Meanwhile, " B " Battery had also swung into action. One of the guns was hit and several vehicles damaged, but eventually a smoke screen was fired to enable all the vehicles to withdraw. The guns kept up fire until the enemy had been silenced, then covered one another out. " B " Battery O.P. registered a fire plan for a set piece attack upon the enemy column but when the tanks and infantry arrived on the objective they found only knocked-out guns and a number of German graves.

A Regimental position was formed behind the Ramal escarpment. " E " Battery sent guns to make up deficiencies in 2nd R.H.A., " B " Battery and the remaining troop of " E " Battery went under command of Major Blacker, whose Battery—" H " Battery, 2nd R.H.A.— was also down to four guns.

" E " Battery H.Q. at Aslagh.

"A" Battery, still in support of The Bays and 6th Royal Tank Regiment in a mobile role guarding the left flank, had been perpetually in action supporting the tanks with observed fire.

The only Regimental target of the whole battle was fired in this position. An O.P. officer of each Battery was shown his section of the large column of enemy forming up to attack the Knightsbridge box. Registration was completed and when the concentration was fired the enemy column was enveloped in shellfire and dispersed.

About this time Lt.-Col. Vaughan Hughes left the Regiment and was succeeded by the 2nd i/c, Major W. M. Leggatt. " E " Battery were now supporting 4th City of London Yeomanry with one O.P. inside the Knightsbridge box, thus favourably placed to help deal with the continuous attacks. The period of comparative inaction which followed the British success was ending and by 11th June the Germans, once again on the offensive, had penetrated the main defensive position in several places. The two chief obstacles left were Bir Hacheim and the Knightsbridge box.

On 11th June it was discovered that the enemy was pushing forward a strong armoured drive towards El Adem and in the evening the group moved towards Bir Lifa to stop this threat. "A" Battery were engaged all day in a violent tank battle, " E " Battery were in action and " B " Battery on the move at 15.00 hours when, passing through 4th City of London Yeomanry group echelon, they were heavily dive-bombed by Ju. 87's and 88's. The bombing had appalling results for " B " Battery, the infantry and anti-tank gunners ; there were very heavy casualties and many vehicles were destroyed. B.S.M. Thorns, S/Sgt. Goodman and Bdr. Parry, three stalwarts of the Battery, were among those who were lost, the first two killed, Bdr. Parry reported missing.

At. 17.00 hours the enemy attack was pressed with great ferocity. The guns fired incessantly. Tanks were urged on by their C.O., Lt.-Col. Frank Arkwright, standing on top of his turret. The enemy were held until dusk, by which time the armour had been forced to withdraw until only 200 yards in front of the Regiment's guns, now subjected to perpetual fire, including armour-piercing shot. The climax came when 90th Light drove up in half-tracks and debussed on the left rear. In the fading light, the guns were swung round to engage the infantry. At nightfall close leaguers were formed with the enemy within 1,000 yards on both sides.

" B " Battery had withdrawn a little earlier in order to reorganise after their serious losses in the bombing. After an uncomfortable night the other guns escaped by a miracle of good fortune and magnificent driving, and by morning on the 13th June were again in action behind the Ramal escarpment, firing at enemy tanks advancing on a wide front. " B " Battery reorganised under Major Hopkins and to the surprise of the Divisional Commander and the staff were in action again that morning.

In the early afternoon a powerful enemy tank column was reported bearing down from the west—in exactly the opposite direction from the main battle of the last two days. The guns were turned round 180 degrees, O.P.s quickly deployed, while tanks raced back to ward off the surprise attack. The enemy tanks first met and overran the Rigel box and then closed towards " B " Battery. British prisoners taken in the box were forced to walk ahead of the tanks. Suddenly, as though someone had given a pre-arranged signal, the prisoners raced away to the flanks and nearly all of them escaped. " B " Battery with O.P.s on the left and on the right, maintained fire until the tanks reined back at about 1,000 yards—by now between the O.Ps. and the Battery.

Bir Hacheim had already fallen and it was decided to evacuate the Guards box that night. Four City of London Yeomanry leaguered nearby to help. They were attacked all night by the light of burning Crusaders and vehicles and by first light had lost approximately half their original tanks.

The three Batteries were once again successfully extricated. Next morning they went into action independently to find that they were close to one another in a perfect Regiment deployment. " E " on the left near Pt. 186, " B" on the right between the Worcesters' box and the South African box at Eluet el Tamar, and "A" echeloned back with The Bays guarding the left flank.

" E " Battery opened fire on 12 Mark IVs, at 1,600 yards. The tanks sat back hull-down while machine-gunners closed in to rake the gun position with fire. A Honey tank on the position was set on fire and the Battery had many casualties. Two tanks were knocked out in return. At midday the " E " Battery troop was ordered to withdraw. The guns first covered the withdrawal of the Rifle Brigade 6-pounder anti-tank guns and then smoked themselves out. The quads raced up under the smoke screen and the position was evacuated without further casualties. The Battery went into action again on the Acroma ridge.

"B" Battery fought a desperate open sight battle after the Worcesters' box had been overrun. Both Capt. Maclaren and the Padre, Capt. Oliver, picked up many escaping Worcester infantry in front of the German tanks. These tanks, having dealt with the box, rushed a minefield which was practically if not completely dummy, and formed a half circle round the guns. "F" Troop had three guns in action on the right, with four guns of "E" Troop a little further back round a bend in the wadi. Orders were to hold the El Tamar ridge for an indefinite time so that the South Africans and elements of 50th Division could be withdrawn from the Gazala sector along the coast road to Tobruk. The guns remained in position facing some 30 German tanks. There had not been time to dig in properly. The Command Post was established in a disused vehicle pit and there Lieut. Kemp, the G.P.O., grounded his wireless set. All vehicles were moved back about one mile to a shallow depression.

One of "B" Battery's three derelict guns destroyed and over-run at Bir el Tamar (Knightsbridge). Photographed in November, 1942, during the advance from El Alamein.

The whole Battery area was covered in successive counter-battery concentrations, and then the tanks opened up from their hull-down firing positions. As first one gun and then another took up the fight so the tanks methodically picked off the gun betrayed by its flash. While tanks on one side machine-gunned the detachment another troop from the other side shot A.P. and H.E. Fire was returned and some six tanks were claimed as hit before the three guns were utterly smashed. Even then the detachments did not leave the guns. No orders to evacuate had been received. Therefore every one sat tight and the tanks were clearly afraid to close in.

Sgt. Deakin, No. 1 of E Sub, had been killed and two other gunners wounded, while the G.P.O. had been very seriously hit. L/Bdr. Bolsom, the G.P.O.A., kept open the command-post wireless and eventually received orders to organise evacuation on foot, under a smoke screen fired by "A" Battery which Major McDermid directed from an O.P. on a bir just behind " B's " guns. As the " F " Troop gunners came out Major Hopkins drove forward to pick them up in his armoured car. He was killed by A.P. shot which also wounded members of his crew.

" E " Troop were now in an exposed position although only one gun and the command-post could see the enemy tanks because of the configuration of the ground. Lieut Sewell, the G.P.O., kept the Troop at " tank-alert " but the German tanks did not close in.

Late in the afternoon orders came through from Brigade to evacuate the position and move due north, the ridge having been held and German armour kept at bay for the required time. Again "A" Battery fired a smoke screen. The quads raced up to " E " Troop. Three of the guns and all the gunners were brought out safely. One quad and gun were destroyed by direct hits as the gun was being limbered up. The remnants of " B " Battery were then collected and withdrawn about two miles where a section was again put into action and immediately opened fire at tanks.

The Bays had engaged enemy armour on the flank and "A" Battery maintained unceasing fire which discouraged the enemy and knocked out several tanks. Capt. Dunn directed fire until he was compelled to withdraw, wounded and with his tank damaged. Major McDermid then leapfrogged the guns back. Two of them were hit and badly damaged, while the breech block of F Sub jammed with the heat caused by so much firing. Major McDermid and the Battery O.P. continued to fire until nightfall, when the result of the day's battle could be seen in a semicircle of burning enemy tanks.

The remnants of "A" and " B " Batteries and Tactical Regimental Headquarters then leaguered with 1st Rifle Brigade. Lt.-Col. Bosville issued orders for a night march to escape from the German forces which surrounded the column on all sides except the north, where the Acroma escarpment barred escape to the coast road. Nevertheless it was resolved to risk the escarpment rather than be captured. A Rifle Brigade officer went down the escarpment on foot and returned with a report that there was a slight chance of success. The column then drove to the lip of the escarpment. Gunners dismounted and with picks and shovels literally hewed and made a tortuous track down the cliff face.

The guns, tanks and other vehicles began the descent, bumping over boulders and jagged rocks all the way down and eventually reached a narrow gully which wound like a ribbon of silver at the foot of the escarpment. When the vehicles reached this wadi everyone was dismayed to discover there was an ascent on the other side up a cliff face with a gradient of about one in two.

Some of the vehicles were on tow. Undaunted the drivers engaged bottom gear and bucketed up the cliff face. So steep was the climb that at times the bonnets were silhouetted over the top of the escarpment. The column reached the top and in a slight mist began another steep descent down a winding track forged through a sort of fine red clay. As dawn broke, the vehicles, many limping with broken springs, patched up, some on tow, but not one missing, reached the plain bordering the coast road. Turning east they were just in time to catch up with the rearguard of the South African column pulling into Tobruk. As the column reached the military cemetery it was fired on by German tanks which had pursued along the top of the escarpment.

The Royal Air Force umbrella prevented the Luftwaffe causing great havoc among the congested vehicles which moved that day to Tobruk. The Regiment carried on to El Adem, pausing only to brew near Acroma and to collect stocks at the bulk N.A.A.F.I. on the El Adem road beyond Tobruk. Then on again to Gambut where Brigadier Briggs, commanding

2nd Armoured Brigade visited the Batteries to express congratulations. Next day the whole of the Brigade group marched further east to Sollum.

Meanwhile the " E " Battery Troop had withdrawn down the Acroma track into Tobruk. There they filled up with petrol. As they left to rejoin the Regiment the Germans had already started to close in on Tobruk. The troop managed to get clear and rejoin the Regiment on the Bardia road next day.

## 4. Way Back

ON 17TH JUNE WHAT REMAINED OF THE REGIMENT concentrated at Sollum. " B " and " E " Batteries again formed a composite Battery and this, together with "A" Battery, went into dug-in positions in the Sollum box. The weather was exhausting but the gunners were able to bathe from the lovely sands in the bay.

For six days while the Germans were attacking Tobruk things were comparatively quiet. Several regimental raiding parties went out and

**Descending Halfaya.**

fought some armoured cars to obtain stores left in the Capuzzo N.A.A.F.I. After the fall of Tobruk it was decided to withdraw, since the German column had outflanked Sollum and the Regiment headed west directed upon Mersa Metruh. To avoid unpleasant contact, the column slipped out of Sollum and took a southern sweep through the desert to reach Matruh on 25th June. Many reinforcements—officers and other ranks—had been posted to the Regiment during the fighting but Batteries were far below strength owing to their heavy casualties. Serious though these casualties were, those in the next phase at Mersa Matruh were even worse and it was during this time that most of those taken prisoner were lost.

Major McDermid commanded "A" Battery and Capt. Armstrong took over the joint " B " and " E " Batteries when the guns occupied dug-in positions in the south-west corner of the Matruh box. For the first time in the whole battle the Battery positions were surveyed in.

On the evening of 26th June, the Regiment was ordered to move 20 kilometres east and then turn south to join up with 167th Brigade of 50th Division. As the column moved south three Bren carriers coming the other way stopped with the news that the enemy was just in front. An uncomfortable night was spent in close leaguer with bursts of small arms fire coming in among the vehicles. When dawn broke Batteries found themselves facing a 105 millimetre position at short range. Leaguer was broken in great haste and positions occupied on a narrow ledge of the escarpment. The O.P.s reported a battalion of 50th Division being marched off in a column. Throughout the day the enemy shelled the positions, but most of their rounds fell 100 yards short. That evening a large enemy column moved round at top speed to the east under heavy fire from the Batteries. Everybody realised they were now completely surrounded. At last light, orders came to go out "leaguer-busting." The Regiment moved a short distance and halted between two enemy leaguers—about 600 yards from each—while Bren carriers attacked.

The guns went into action but did not fire. A little later the column moved on again south, having to pass through a defile covered by a 50 millimetre anti-tank gun firing on fixed lines at about 100 yards range. Rounds came over with about four seconds interval, which gave just time for a vehicle to slip past—with good timing. At 01.00 hours the column was clear and halted near an Italian leaguer.

Mystifying orders then came to retrace the route and return. Subsequently it was said the other Brigade had not broken clear. Much the same type of fighting happened on the return. Soon after dawn the Batteries again occupied positions within the perimeter. The "B" Battery Troop had become separated and drove right through an enemy leaguer to rejoin about midday.

Lieut. McAllum was captured by Arabs who thought he was German because he had a number of German papers. They were about to kill him when R.S.M. Dowdney appeared and produced enough Arabic to persuade them they had caught an English officer, and Lieut. McAllum was released.

The Batteries remained that day in action near Garawlah. "A" Battery were heavily engaged by 150-millimetres throughout the day and their casualties included Lieut. Leftwich, who was killed. The enemy closed in until at 18.00 hours the guns were engaging infantry over open sights at 1,200 yards. Soon after dark the remnants of 50th Division formed up in eight separate columns, each one given a different route in a final effort to break out east.

Major McDermid commanded the "A" Battery column, composed of his tank, the H and G trucks and four guns, with one fifteen-hundredweight and three three-tonners. The column moved off at midnight under accurate and heavy Breda and machine-gun fire. Major McDermid was wounded in the eye but L/Bdr. Forster and the crew brought him through safely.

The column simply ran the gauntlet of cross fire, veered away from a particularly aggressive German leaguer and negotiated precipitous wadis, shot at all the way. When those who had got through stopped at first light to bury one of the men who had been killed, Mark IVs opened up with A.P. shot. The column then headed east and touched the edge of the Quattara Depression where the course was changed northwards. On the following morning they joined other vehicles of the Regiment gathering at Hammam Station.

Meanwhile, "B/E" Battery, under Major Armstrong, had moved off in two Troop Groups with the East Yorks and a troop of 6-prs. of the

Norfolk Yeomanry. As the leading column of the Division, they were ordered to burst a way through the enemy position and hold a bridgehead to enable succeeding columns to pass. The East Yorks debussed at the lip of the escarpment under heavy fire and forced an opening on foot and in carriers with Bren and bayonet. The guns and other M.T. passed through under intense close-range fire, but many vehicles were hit and left burning. Brave and great-hearted men were killed that night and many more captured.

Every single man in the Regiment who got through told exciting stories of hand-to-hand fighting. Capt. Maclaren's tank broke down. While doing a reconnaissance on foot he was attacked by Italians wearing red cross armbands and wounded by a grenade. He was picked up by a Northumberland Fusilier fifteen-hundredweight. Lieut. Thomson-Glover's truck, separated from everybody else, met a German column which he and his crew held up. They took a quad and a fifteen-hundredweight and destroyed two three-tonners.

"The Auk" and Officers of "B E" Battery.

By 10.00 hrs. next day Major Armstrong with two guns and Capt. de Boinville with his troop complete met at Galal. For several days stragglers continued to get out through Fuka down the road to Alamein and Amyria. Of the seven 25-pounders which 50th Division got away, six belonged to the Regiment. Fortunately most of the " B " echelon had left Matruh by the coast road just before the road was cut.

General Auchinleck met Major Armstrong on the coast road near El Alamein. " Do you think Eighth Army is beaten ? " he asked. Major Armstrong replied, " Of course not." The General said the army would hold the line between El Alamein and the Quattara Depression.

The Regiment then formed a composite Battery of seven guns and overnight were ordered " to move due west 15 miles, and contact Brigadier Waller, who will need every gun he can get." The Battery duly marched west towards the noise of gunfire and joined " Robcol," coming into action on the right of 1 R.H.A. Certainly every gun, and every shell, was wanted. A mobile battle swung to and fro for some days with the Boche straining every nerve to break through the last barrier to Alex. before his momentum was spent. Finally, " Robcol " and the mixed tank brigade on its southern flank, stiffened by 6-pounders which began to prove their worth at last, dug itself in behind the favourable ground of Ruweisat Ridge, and the remaining enemy armour frittered away in front of it. Eighth Army had made its last ditch stand ; Egypt was saved ; and thereafter until the end of the war no Battery of the Regiment ever withdrew. It is, perhaps, well to recall that this small action was, in fact, the turning point of the war. Once the crisis was past the initiative was ours.

The H.A.C. Battery carried on for about a fortnight under the command of Major Armstrong. Regimental Headquarters was set up at Amyria only a short distance from the camp site where the Regiment had

**Officers of the 11th after the retreat from Knightsbridge to Alamein.**

leaguered fresh from England. A new Regimental Headquarters staff was formed, Capt. Green (Adjutant), who had been captured during the Garawlah breakout, was succeeded by Capt Wathen.

The composite Battery had brought back large quantities of tinned food and crates of beer, cordial and gin. Since the guns were so close to Alexandria an L.O. was sent back for supplies, doing the round trip every two days. Defiant, the gunners fought their guns throughout that first fortnight of July and helped to throw back two more German attacks. They advanced once more before they were relieved. The news may have seemed dismal to the outside world ; there was considerable panic throughout the Delta ; but on the Ruweisat Ridge there was complete confidence, especially as the Australians, New Zealanders, other guns and tanks had arrived to consolidate the line.

There were persistent rumours that 8th Armoured Division and the Highland Division were on their way from England and that the " Queen Mary " was bring 20,000 other reinforcements. For a change rumour was truth. In the middle of July, the Alamein line was strongly held and the Delta safe.

Major Armstrong began the Ruweisat battle with a fever but carried on and gave fine encouragement to the Battery by his leadership ; his " rockets " ensured a high standard of discipline and gunnery. Although the enemy both shelled and dive-bombed the positions at Ruweisat there was only one casualty in the Battery—a gunner slightly burnt by a charge which caught fire. Suddenly the long-awaited code-word came over the Battery net—" Monster aunt sally," which meant relief that night.

The Battery leaguered near El Amayid with the soothing murmur of the Mediterranean rolling on the silvery sand dunes. The next day the guns joined the rest of the Regiment. Celebrations were held in Alexandria, equipment was handed in and the Regiment drove down to the Base Depot, Royal Artillery, at Almaza, Cairo.

★ ★ ★

# PART THREE

## ATTACK : AUGUST, 1942 — MAY, 1943

1. ALAMEIN.
2. TMIMI TO MARETH.
3. LEFT HOOK.
4. END IN AFRICA.

## 1. Alamein

THE PITIFULLY SMALL CONVOY of three-tonners transporting the Regiment arrived at Base Depot, Royal Artillery, towards the end of July. The Regimental spirit was never better reflected than in the turnout and discipline of the men, few though they were, who drove through Cairo that day after so many hardships.

Nearly everybody was sent away on leave, courses were started, high-spirited parties were held in Cairo when other Regiments returned, and the survivors of the O.P. Club formed at Knightsbridge gathered for reunion. Visits were paid to hospitals where members of the Regiment were recovering from their wounds.

Rumours had been afloat of a mysterious new equipment called a self-propelled gun. The Americans had produced this new gun and it was said Mr. Roosevelt promised delivery when he met Mr. Churchill at the time Tobruk had fallen. Nothing further was known about the equipment, nor was it known which Regiment would be first to get the new guns. A memorial service was held in Cairo Cathedral to those of the Regiment who had been killed. In the evening members of the H.A.C. met for a reunion dinner at Shepheard's.

After a few weeks at Base Depot, Royal Artillery, the Regiment moved to Tahag, approximately 12 miles from Ismailia, a return to sand but at any rate the camp had tarmac roads and N.A.A.F.I.s, and in Ismailia there were two clubs and sailing on Lake Timsah. Command changed with astonishing frequency. For a time the Regiment was nominally in 10th Armoured Division but everybody was anxious to return to 1st Armoured Division. On 20th August this hope materialised and the Regiment drove back through Cairo and half-way up the Alexandria road to Khatatba, where Batteries pitched their tents next door to their own armoured Regiments. This created much rejoicing and liaison was reopened at once. The Regiment had a nominal amount of equipment for training and also organised a complete battery under Major Croxton for the defence of the Nile should the Germans break through. Many gun positions were reconnoitred along the road between

Mena House to some five miles north of Halfway House, facing the Quattara Depression, though it was never seriously considered likely that the Germans would attempt to cross this treacherous sea of shifting sand.

Rumours of the self-propelled equipment grew stronger. There was still no information as to the equipment itself save that its code name was "Priest" and that it had a 105 millimetre piece. The climax to all this gossip was the announcement that the Regiment would be equipped with the first delivery from America. Tempering the pride in this decision was the realisation of the responsibility which would devolve upon the Regiment in taking the untried Priest into action for the first time.

These were perhaps the most difficult weeks from a domestic point of view that the Regiment experienced during the war. The conversion to the American Priest establishment involved problems of training, equipment, technical gunnery, tactical handling and supply which had never before been considered, much less tried in battle. The Regiment was, therefore, left very much to its own devices and by trial and error to evolve its own solution. The Americans themselves came forward with typically thorough instructions in the mechanics and maintenance of the new equipment and suggestions regarding the tactical handling. A number of officers, Nos. 1, and drivers were sent to the American School at Heliopolis and given not only a very hospitable reception but a most valuable course of instruction.

When the Priest was produced it was found to be a Grant, the turret removed and a 105 millimetre gun-howitzer installed, with armour-plated sides and a sort of armour-plated pulpit which mounted a .5 Browning A.-A. gun. The equipment was promised by 10th September and, although it was learnt that some of the Priests were lost at sea, the first delivery did in fact arrive at that time.

Batteries began intensive training in maintenance, daily tasks, driving drill, laying and technical gunnery—only one of the many problems was the American method of survey with sights graduated in mils. instead of degrees to which British gunners were accustomed. The gunners learnt a new language of "panoramic telescopes," pro dialsights, "aiming circles," "pro directors" and "radial air-cooled aero engine," pro the un-romantic quad. Many visitors, including the Army Commander, inspected the Priests and watched training in progress. At calibration the O.P.s brought in excellent reports of the shell burst.

There had been some talk about using the Priests as tank-busters over open sights. The American instructors impressed upon the students two important points, viz., the Priest armour-plate was proof only against splinters and small arms and that the piece was a 105 millimetre gun-howitzer with a low muzzle velocity. The Americans, therefore, advised using the Priests exactly as field guns and this was the policy adopted by the Regiment. It was decided to fight the Priests as eight gun batteries divided into two troops in the normal way, that the guns should be sited under cover, that, in short, the Priests should be used as movable gun pits. Because the crews were protected by armour plate and also because, with flashless charges, there was no need to insist upon extensive flash cover in the choice of positions, it was possible to use the Priests well up behind the leading armour with infinitely more safety than 25-pounders had been used in the last battle. The use of a single "winkle" gun to take on machine-gun posts was not overlooked, although it was recommended that positions should be chosen where the Priest itself would be below the crest. The inclusion of a No. 19 wireless set in the AFV. equipment gave rise to many theories on the control of firing and movement. One gunner per detachment was trained as wireless operator.

Experiments were made with wireless, voice control, and a telephone system with lines reeled out from each Priest to the Command Post. For technical and supply reasons it was eventually decided that wireless control was not feasible. Thereafter G.P.O.s relied almost entirely upon the telephone, amplified by the Tannoy system with voice control as necessary.

During this period of upheaval and experiment the Regiment received an influx of approximately 350 reinforcements who had just arrived in the country direct from the United Kingdom. They had sailed as drafts, had a most unpleasant voyage and journey through Egypt and indeed looked very sorry for themselves. None had shorts to fit, all wore topees (which the Regiment had discarded and never worn since arriving in Egypt) and their white knees, white faces and bewildered appearance created an astonishing spectacle.

The old hands welcomed the newcomers to the Batteries, found them accommodation, produced tea and a good meal, then introduced them to the Battery canteens; so that by "lights-out" on the first day the reinforcements were already favourably impressed with their new Regiment. Sorting out, re-clothing and settling down, interviews and the allocation of suitable jobs continued for a few days and then another

New "Honeys" (O.P.'s) at Quassassin.

New "Honeys" (O.P.'s) at Quassassin, September, 1942.

miracle had happened within the Regiment, for the newcomers had absorbed the spirit peculiar to their Batteries and, except that they still wore topees, were almost indistinguishable from the old members. When at last their topees were abandoned they felt they had been finally inducted into the Regiment. The warrant officers and non-commissioned officers had rendered a remarkable service both to the Regiment and to the reinforcements by inculcating the Regimental doctrines and by consideration for each man's problems, blended with the enforcement of good discipline.

Many officers were required to fill the places of the nineteen killed and captured and several of those who had been wounded. This was in itself a trial and was aggravated at Khatatba by the departure of Major Armstrong and five other officers after a domestic crisis. Vacancies were filled by senior ranks just out from England and by junior officers recently commissioned from O.C.T.U. Only two of the newcomers had previous service in the Regiment. Lieut.-Col. Leggatt was the C.O., and Major J. R. Richmond, T.D., arrived as second in command; Major Hankey to command "A"; while Major Maclaren and Major Croxton commanded " B " and " E," respectively, with Capt. Wathen as Adjutant.

Although the reinforcement officers were for the most part strangers to one another they quickly settled down and set about learning the new problems of the Priest. Re-equipment with the new type of guns threw extra work on the L.A.D. commanded by Lieut. Norwood and also resulted in an appointment which had already existed in the cavalry regiments, the post of Technical Adjutant. Capt. Page was a most fortunate choice, for he had the requisite knowledge on the mechanical side.

Regimental training developed into Brigade and Divisional schemes when night marches, negotiation of minefields along taped lanes and deployment in action on the other side were practised in the secrecy of the desert between Khatatba and Tababi. The shape of things to come materialised from the frequent practices of minefield breaking. A sensation of supreme confidence was strengthened by the delivery of the new 75-millimetre Sherman tanks to the cavalry. Everybody waited impatiently for the battle for Egypt which was obviously not far off. Rommel had made an abortive armoured attack and General Montgomery was now preparing to open the great offensive from El Alamein.

No written orders for these operations were ever issued to Batteries, nor as far as can be ascertained to the Regiment. Instead, a series of conferences was held where points of training were discussed, lessons driven home and gradually the plan was revealed. No details of the actual operations were released until a few hours before the battle began on 23rd October.

On the morning of 20th October, the Regiment split up into two groups—wheels and tracks—a method of travel which was to become so familiar during all future operations. A Regimental echelon area was formed, for it was decided to take only a small supply echelon into battle behind the Priests. The guns moved off on the first stage of an ambitious deception plan. An enormous concentration of armour was built up in an area behind the line south of the Ruweisat ridge. Tanks and guns moved into leaguer by night. German reconnaisance planes flew over and although shot at were allowed to go back with the news. Sappers built canvas screens over the exact places where tanks and guns stood and by night the real tanks and guns stole away to another concentration area in the north.

The area thus vacated looked very much alive, for native troops were kept there to light brew fires, create a litter of equipment, while the imitation tanks were indistinguishable from real ones at 20 yards.

The Germans were thus led to believe that a huge concentration of armour was being amassed for an attack in the south, whereas in reality the armour was concentrated in the north. There, in the El Hammam area, near the place where the guns had leaguered on their relief from Ruweisat in July, a bogus camp had been assembled during the past month or more.

This camp consisted of canvas screens representing tanks and vehicles, which the Germans knew to be a dummy concentration. During the three nights preceding Alamein real tanks stole up, positioned themselves under these screens and after they had obliterated all tracks the crews were ordered to remain under cover. There seemed to be no change in the camp and it was hoped that reconnaissance planes would be deceived into thinking the assembly area still deserted.

During the afternoon of 23rd October all the officers were called to Brigade Headquarters, and the plan was outlined by Brigadier Fisher, who also read General Montgomery's inspiring message.

Lieut.-Col. Leggatt amplified the orders and the whole of this information was transmitted to all ranks. Maps with an overprint of all known German defences and minefields were issued throughout the Batteries. All ranks knew not only the dispositions of their own troops and the enemy but the exact plan of the operation. For the first time the people who were going to fight the battle were really " in the picture."

Dispositions before the battle were as follows. The enemy held a line from the coast to the Quattara Depression protected by belts of minefields running north-south, with another minefield running east-west through the centre designed to prevent any armoured breakthrough from joining up and thus turning the line. 21st Panzer, 90th Light and Trieste Armoured Divisions with 164th Infantry Divisions were disposed in the northern half ; 15th Panzer and Ariete Armoured Division in the south, with German and Italian infantry divisions holding the forward positions. The country was for the most part flat except for a feature known as Kidney Ridge and Tel el Aquaqir which ran more or less parallel with and behind the main German defended localities.

The British line extended from the Hill of Jesus, just beyond El Alamein, across Ruweisat Ridge to Haminat on the lip of the Quattara Depression, and was held by the Australians on the right, the New Zealanders, 51st Highland Division, South African Division, 50th Division, 44th Division, Greek Brigade and Free French. The armour consisted of 1st, 7th, and 10th Armoured Divisions, 4th Light Armoured Brigade, and a number of Army tank and independent Brigades.

General Montgomery's plan was to make an infantry attack north of Ruweisat Ridge, pass the armour through and secure Kidney Ridge, to keep off and destroy the enemy armour while the infantry fought a battle of attrition. Meanwhile, it was appreciated, the German east-west minefield would handicap the movement of enemy armour from the south to the northern sector.

The attack was to be made under the most concentrated barrage yet known, with one gun for every 23 yards of the front. The Desert Air Force had guaranteed fighter cover and close bombing support, while strategic bombing would be carried out in depth.

The rôle of 2nd Armoured Brigade, which with 7th Motor Brigade, composed 1st Armoured Division, was to go through 51st Highland Division. Even if the British lost one tank for every German tank knocked out there was still enough armour left to win; in fact, it was said that, including the tanks in the line, those in forward delivery squadrons and at base, there was a three to one British supremacy. Whether or not this was true, for the first time the type of tank in use was superior to the Germans'. The Sherman with its 75-millimetre gun proved tougher, more powerful and more manœuvrable than the German Mark III and Mark IV. The Italian M.13 was of course so much papier mâché.

Just before last light on 23rd October, Battery Commanders and O.P.s joined their regiments and squadrons and the guns formed up ready to move into battle. 2nd Armoured Brigade was to advance along three tracks—Sun, Moon and Star—which were to be continued through the enemy minefields where white tapes and direction lamps could mark lanes cleared by Sappers advancing with the infantry. Each armoured group had something special by way of an eve of Waterloo celebration. The final toast was drunk as the moon rose.

At about 20.45 hours, the columns moved out into single file on their respective tracks and there halted. The moon rose high over the silent battlefield and a single German aeroplane flew overhead. In the still silence the beat of its engine was heard approaching miles away, then the sudden whistle of a bomb which fell near the 2nd Armoured Brigade group. The bomb did no damage—it only put everyone into the proper frame of mind.

Silence again until 22.00 hours; when the whole world suddenly exploded. Flashes of flame tore the sky from 800 guns firing into the German lines and the crack and rumble of gunfire echoed across the desert where a million men were standing to.

The tank columns started up and moved forward in three regimental groups 100 yards apart, up through the medium guns, then the 25-pounders. Gunners who were resting waved "God-speed." After a halt to refill tanks the armour churned forward again, creating a tremendous volume of dust which fortunately was blown away by a cross wind. All the tank commanders were nevertheless soon caked with sand and their eyes encrusted as they peered out over the minefields where in the eerie darkness the enemy might suddenly appear.

The Corps of Military Police provided traffic control sentries whose work was carried out with efficiency and great personal bravery. Searchlights rose in the north and the south as "trig points" to which compass

*Crown Copyright reserved.*

**The 11th H.A.C. at El Alamein.**

bearings could be taken to check positions and as a further aid to direction. Bofors guns fired bursts of tracer to mark the boundaries of the advancing battalions.

Small arms fire crackled and tracer flew across the sky. Ambulances and stretcher parties brought back wounded and now batches of prisoners—dazed, unkempt, many in their nightclothes—were being collected and marched back. In the distance Royal Air Force bombers dropped hanging flares. Barbed wire and silent forms and dust and still the tanks went on and on while the moon dropped slowly towards the west.

The guns were not yet clear of the mine field, with the moon still hanging above the horizon, when the first 88-millimetre shells landed among the leading tanks which had just emerged from the second German minefield. According to the timetable the leading squadrons should have been through the third minefield by dawn. They were 500 yards short when dawn broke; before anybody had much time to think it was broad daylight and the battle had begun in earnest.

On the left enemy infantry held a strongpoint. Anti-tank guns were hidden on the slopes which arose in front of Kidney Ridge. Field guns behind the ridge were firing into the most extraordinary target their O.P.s had ever seen, a vast army of tanks, guns and vehicles packed into the German minefields.

Within a few minutes all the Regiment's O.P.s were calling for fire and the Batteries deployed in the only possible way behind their regiments. They simply turned off the track into the minefield. But the risk, once accepted, proved astonishingly small, for not a single Priest or vehicle suffered real damage from the mines.

During that morning the guns shot troop targets, G.F. targets, enemy guns now firing and enemy infantry. There was hardly a moment when they were not firing. There was so much the Germans could shoot at that they could not distinguish the Batteries firing among the conglomeration of tanks and vehicles covered by the rolling fog of war and none of the gun positions was accurately pin-pointed, although shells were falling everywhere indiscriminately—as indeed they continued to do throughout the whole battle.

*Crown Copyright reserved.*

**A " Priest " loading up with petrol.**

The Germans had been shattered by the counter-battery, bombing, barrage and infantry attack, but they had still plenty of armour as a mobile counter-attack force, undamaged guns and dogged infantry holding out both behind the leading British tanks and dug in ahead of them.

All three cavalry regiments were using their 75-millimetre guns which blasted enemy tanks, and especially the M.13s, so that within a few hours there was a ring of burning tanks on the slopes ahead, while tanks and vehicles burnt here and there in the British lines.

At midday it was announced that the Highlanders would attack again, since they had not secured the final objectives during the night. That afternoon, in blazing sunshine, those magnificent Scotsmen got to their feet and with their bayonets glittering walked forward indifferent to the shells falling among them. The attack gained momentum and they finished with a charge at the double to gain 800 yards of ground. They used their bayonets for the infighting which developed as they entered German company positions to capture the third minefield. This was believed to be the final minefield before the open ground in front of Kidney Ridge, but two more were discovered when the first tanks through the third minefield fanned out beyond and immediately had casualties on mines.

Over on the right The Queen's Bays supported by "A" Battery were engaged in a tank battle to stop an immediate counter-attack. When the enemy appeared, "A" Battery was ordered to charge forward, engage over open sights at 3,000 yards, closing to 1,800 yards. The Bays' Shermans were deployed just ahead. Meeting the pitiless fire from terrifying Shermans and Priests the enemy faltered and drew away into the gathering darkness, leaving a number of burning tanks. The Battery was then ordered to a more concealed position. Two men were killed and the Battery Commander's tank blown up on a mine with the result that Major Hankey and all his crew were evacuated wounded. Major Chrimes took over command of "A" Battery.

That night the guns remained where they were while the O.P.s leaguered with the in-squadrons, leaguers which were harassed by machine guns firing on fixed lines and by Ju. 88s.

" H " Troop Command Post, El Alamein.

All next day the battle continued in very much the same way, culminating with an attack by 9th Lancers in the afternoon. The O.P.s of all three Batteries were continually engaged neutralising anti-tank guns, harassing the tanks, and all three Batteries claimed considerable destruction.

For the first time the Batteries were shooting airburst and bouncing H.E. shells to give airburst only a few feet above the ground. These shells were particularly effective against troops in slit trenches and were also fired beyond crests when movement was betrayed by dust clouds rising from the wadis. All O.Ps. reported brews from shoots of this type and everybody developed the highest opinion of airbursts dotting the sky with black curling puffs that spat venom in their very appearance.

All Batteries had direct hits on their guns from 88-millimetre H.E. and 105-millimetre shells. Gun crews showed great bravery under the gusts of fire for, although the armour plating was protection for crews inside the Priests, the men had to take turns at ammunition duties on the ground. In these circumstances they learnt to brew up in slit trenches behind the Priest where there was more protection from shellfire and machine gunning.

By night the infantry carried out further attacks to improve their positions. The general attack was going well, if slowly, but the enemy had concentrated his armour on the Brigade's front and the two sides were locked in merciless fighting.

It is impossible to detail incidents on the successive days. All Batteries had similar experiences, suffered casualties, but kept up continuous support to the tanks during the day, while at night the field and medium guns opened up their fusilade in support of infantry attacks.

On 25th October, the whole Regiment fired in a joint fire plan with 2nd and 4th R.H.A. and 78th Field Regiment, to support a cavalry charge by " C " Squadron of 10th Hussars. Earlier in the battle " C " Squadron had made one charge towards Kidney Ridge as a demonstration. The purpose of the charge on the 25th was to make a flanking attack upon the ridge and if possible draw away enemy armour which was heavily attacking the Brigade's next door neighbours on the left. " C " Squadron's objective was an anti-tank gun position which was also the Regiment's target in the fire plan; 9th Lancers and The Queen's Bays helped to lay smoke screens. As the fire plan came down, " C " Squadron charged through the fourth minefield and had 600 yards to go when the first tank hit the fifth minefield. The squadron wheeled to the right and found a way round, heading straight for the objective.

" B " Battery's F.O.O. ordered " cease fire " and the tanks went in. Until that moment there had been no reply from the enemy. When the fire plan stopped, anti-tank guns sited in enfilade opened up and quickly knocked out five Shermans. The F.O.O. ordered a repeat of the fire plan and as the shellfire came down the remainder of " C " Squadron withdrew in safety. Much valuable information was gained, enemy armour was drawn away from the left, several anti-tank guns were knocked out.

That night the Gordon Highlanders on the right of the Brigade were directed upon the Kidney feature, while the Australians were to attack in the direction of Tommy's Fort in the north. Kidney Ridge was captured and the Rifle Brigade, installing themselves in the " Snipe " position, fought one of the most brilliant actions of the whole war, in which their C.O., Lt.-Col. Vic Turner, won the V.C.

Anti-tank guns which the Rifle Brigade had taken on to " Snipe " knocked out wave after wave of counter-attacking tanks. When the Brigade occupied the commanding feature of the ridge their Sherman tanks also joined in knocking out more German and Italian tanks, thus finally writing off the main armoured counter-attack from the north.

All O.P.s had exciting shooting from Kidney Ridge and the Batteries, moving forward, caused great havoc among the enemy's gun lines and infantry positions. O.P.s were learning to call for D.A.F. support. Successive waves of Boston bombers which plastered acres of the enemy's lines were most invigorating to watch. Several times O.P.s were able to obtain the services of a " tea-party " upon suitable enemy concentrations.

The Batteries registered a battery of six 88-millimetres and every time the Desert Air Force appeared one of the Batteries took on the 88-millimetres in an effort to keep them quiet which met with a reasonable amount of success.

On the evening of 28th October, the Regiment was withdrawn with 2nd Armoured Brigade for a short rest. The Batteries drove back along the minefield tracks, past fresh infantry going in, past burnt out vehicles, past the guns firing the barrage for another attack, drove through swirling powdered sand following the tiny amber and green lights, back beyond El Alamein, until at last the Priests pulled off the track and halted. The gunners flung themselves down and slept. Battery parades were held next day, all equipment checked, repairs, maintenance carried out and then another long night's sleep.

Next morning officers were called to Brigade Headquarters for a conference. No one expected congratulations, but everyone was in high spirits, for the Brigade had supported the infantry on to their objectives, had destroyed the anti-tank defences and knocked out the best part of the armoured forces the enemy had used on that sector. Officers sat round in a circle, waiting. Nothing that could be said could have created more surprise than the Brigadier's first words. " Gentlemen," he said, " the situation is desperate." He went on to say that the Brigade was going in again behind a New Zealand attack, slightly north of and parallel to the first one. The objective was the line of telegraph posts and north-south supply route just beyond Tel el Aquaqir. " The Brigade must reach this objective, and we are prepared to accept 80% casualties—only our tanks must get there." Those were the orders and the Brigadier hinted that this offensive was meant to tie up with strategy on a high level. What that was no one knew until some days later when the B.B.C. announced that the 1st Army had landed in North Africa.

That night was a replica of the first night of the attack at Alamein— the same organisation of the white taped lanes, the same barrage, the same noise, the same columns of tanks and guns, except that this time the sand churned up by the tank in front was blown back by a headwind, stinging into the faces of those behind. The moon rose and then dropped into the west, just as on that other first morning, and the dawn brought the same crash of enemy shellfire.

There was a slight mist and through it plodded the New Zealanders, great fighting infantry, advancing to their objectives. The British tanks surprised dug-in M.13s. and the 75-millimetres cracked, destroying the enemy tanks in their pits. A dozen Mark IIIs. and Mark IVs. wheeled punch-drunk on the ridge 1,000 yards away ; every one was knocked out, the last but one in the column stopped to help another and was immediately brewed by two Shermans.

Firing and bounding forward, troop covering troop, seeking what little cover could be found in shallow wadis, the three Regiments spilled forward up the sloping desert into the anti-tank defences. The Bays ran into an anti-tank gun layout and Capt. Watt, who had transferred to "A" Battery as Troop Commander only the previous day, was killed when his tank was hit. His crew later returned with 12 Italian prisoners.

On the left a brigade of tanks had run upon serious trouble. On the right, it was reported, the Australians were giving the Germans hell near Tommy's Fort. Next day the telegraph posts were in full view some few thousands of yards away.

For the Batteries it was the same sort of battle as before, firing on strong-points, neutralising anti-tank guns, shooting up vehicles wherever movement was seen. And once again the cavalry gleefully watched airburst curling above the enemy lines.

The Desert Air Force still kept up a continuous service of Boston tea-parties ; fighters wheeled overhead and enemy planes only occasionally dived in to bomb the gun lines. When this happened the gunners usually saw exciting aerial battles in which the Desert Air Force fighters always shot down a good proportion of Stukas and other aircraft. Nevertheless several ammunition trucks were destroyed by bombing with a few casualties.

The ninth day of the battle seemed easier and the leading tanks, with the infantry, had not very far to go to the top of the crest. General Montgomery had said that if the offensive was maintained without respite the enemy could not last more than ten days, and now there were signs that resistance was failing. Late that afternoon, away on the left, two Shermans edged round a small feature and crossed the telegraph line. That night the tanks did not withdraw the customary 100 yards or so to leaguer but formed up on the battlefield where they had been fighting. Just after sundown the Batteries were given cease fire and ordered to drive up to their respective regimental leaguers.

In leaguer that night there was much discussion of reports that the Royal Air Force had seen continuous streams of German transport heading west. During the night the 25-pounders fired a heavy barrage, and as the gunners lay near their Priests they heard the shells whistling overhead to fall on the start line only about 200 yards beyond the leaguer.

There was mist the next morning ; to increase the confusion the

*Crown Copyright reserved.*

**A " Priest " of the 11th H.A.C. in pursuit of the Afrika Corps.**

25-pounders put down smoke as the infantry went in over the top of the hill across the plateau to their objectives. Regiments broke leaguer, wheeled round and drove through the enemy positions—not without an occasional mishap among the vehicle pits in the fog. Scotsmen were milling around the dugouts and abandoned equipment and vehicles. The tanks pushed on—over the telegraph wires and the Brigade was through.

The relief and tremendous spirit of jubilation were terrific. More tanks were conforming on the left of the line. Orders were given to push on and the regiments therefore drove forward, followed by their Batteries in desert formation. Leaving the debris of the beaten army behind, the Brigade drove steadily forward and advanced six miles, when the leading tanks crashed heavily into a rearguard of tanks and anti-tank guns. All three Batteries took up the challenge, firing to the north, west and south-west at tanks, anti-tank guns and supply vehicles surprised in what they had imagined to be their own territory. The Brigade was firmly established behind the German lines.

10th Hussars tanks knocked out a German Mark III. which came alone over the sand dunes. The commander and crew baled out but were pinned to the ground by the H.E. bursts. Firing stopped and a tall figure in black dungarees walked slowly towards the attacking tanks. He was evidently someone of importance from the red and gold facings which could be distinguished on his uniform; in addition he was wearing binoculars enormous by German standards, even although they always went in for binoculars twice as big as the British pattern.

A scout car darted forward racing the O.P. tank, everybody bent on getting those glasses. Capt. Grant Singer, commander of 10th Hussars reconnaissance troop, stood in the dingo. As he stopped the tall, dark figure halted, saluted smartly, and shook hands. He was General Von Thoma, commanding the Afrika Korps in the absence of Rommel. Everyone was so excited that Von Thoma was sent back still wearing his binoculars. Von Thoma said later that the destruction of the anti-tank guns and armour on this sector was the primary tactical cause of the German defeat.

By the end of the day the Brigade had penetrated ten miles. Next morning the regiments charged forward a further 20 miles, turning in a northerly direction. At 08.00 hours the Brigade met another rearguard which was overcome after a short fight of about an hour, in which Capt. Butler-Stoney, who had taken over " E " Battery after Major Croxton was wounded at Aqquaqir, directed fire from " E " Battery on to two 88-millimetre guns which were concealed behind a crest and had knocked out several of the leading tanks. "A" and " B " joined in the concentration, which was so fierce and accurate, that the enemy rearguard was spread-eagled and overrun.

The Brigade headed north to the sea. On the way German supply lorries were captured with considerable booty of which the Batteries had their full share, and finally the Brigade cut the coast road west of Daba. Here the Batteries noticed with bitterness that the Germans had destroyed the famous " Noah's Ark " N.A.A.F.I.

Turning west the Brigade overran a huge German armoured workshop which had previously been shelled by the Navy. A few miles farther on a Royal Air Force column drove through the Regiment heading steadily west. Most of the trucks were stopped and the few which carried on soon came back at considerable speed. This incident illustrates how keen were the Royal Air Force to push forward and develop aerodromes, thus maintaining close fighter support.

In the afternoon the Brigade halted to reform and the Batteries learnt they would get no sleep that night. The Brigade marched through the night south across the desert with the intention of making a wide sweep round Mersa Matruh into the rear of 90th Light near Charing Cross.

Next day the weather broke and a manœuvre which would have altered the whole war in Africa was ruined. Rain poured down all day and by the afternoon tanks made very heavy going through deep mud. Miserable though everybody felt, there was scarcely a soul in the Regiment who did not feel more sorry for the plight of a long column of Italian prisoners, six deep, marching up from the south. They were part of the Italian forces abandoned in the south of the line by Germans who took all available transport to move their own men. This line of prisoners was a whole division with the General marching at its head on his way to surrender at Fuka.

By sundown the Brigade were near Bir Kalda some 15 miles south of the Matruh-Sidi Barrani road. Rain and mud had slowed down the advance of the tanks which then leaguered waiting for the echelons to replenish.

Alas! No supply echelons could get through the desert transformed into a marsh.

A composite squadron of 9th Lancers with " E " Battery, had been able to get a little way further forward, only to be perhaps more bitterly disappointed than the rest of the Brigade for, from the edge of the high plateau, their O.P.s looked down on the tremendous concentration of transport which represented 90th Light and other elements of the Afrika Korps. The German vehicles were also practically out of petrol. Their consternation must have been very great when this tank force suddenly appeared on their flank, and it is impossible to gauge their wonderment when the tanks did not advance among them.

The tanks and " E " Battery had only five miles of petrol in their tanks—insufficient to get down the escarpment and cross the desert to the concentration, never mind manœuvre and fight. The Germans sent out frantic appeals to the Luftwaffe which were answered when the " E " Battery group was severely dive-bombed and strafed.

" E " Battery at Mersa Matruh, 9th November, 1942.

Supplies arrived for 90th Light next day and they made away astride the main road. On the following day, after a break of 48 hours, echelons got through the mud flats and once again the Brigade drove forward converging upon the aerodrome west of Mersa Matruh. During this march through the desert many burnt-out Grant tanks were found in the positions where they had been knocked out during the fighting near Matruh in the previous June.

9th Lancers from one flank and 10th Hussars from the other charged a light defensive screen to overrun the aerodrome. The whole Division then concentrated in the area while the general advance carried on. On 7th November the B.B.C. broadcast news of the 1st Army's landing in North Africa and the Regiment was impatient to get on and reach Tripoli first.

It was believed that the Brigade would be ordered to sweep across the desert along the track followed in December, 1941, to reach the El Agheila line before the German forces could withdraw from Tobruk through the Djebel, out of Benghazi and beyond. This plan did not materialise because, it was said, sufficient petrol could not be obtained—but there was never any official confirmation of this story. At any rate the Division stayed in the Matruh area until news was received that Tobruk had fallen. The tanks and Priests were then loaded on transporters and the Regiment moved with 2nd Armoured Brigade along the coast road west to Sollum, up the winding Halfaya Pass, from the top of which one could see streams of vehicles, three deep, all the way back to the horizon.

On again through Fort Capuzzo, over the ground which evoked so many memories of the withdrawal only four months ago, on through Gambut to El Adem. From El Adem parties went from each of the Batteries to Tobruk and to the Knightsbridge battlefield, which was discovered to be in exactly the same condition as it had been left in June. The enemy had apparently moved across the battlefield and never returned, for the Trigh Capuzzo was overgrown with camel thorn and the ruts had caked hard. On one of these pilgrimages a " B " Battery jeep followed the course back from the Tamar ridge and crossed the Acroma escarpment through the two piles of marker stones just to make sure it really was possible.

Weather had now broken for the winter and in the rain, while 7th Armoured Division and 51st Highland Division carried on the pursuit, 1st Armoured Division was transported through Gazala to a stretch of desert between Tmimi and Rotunda Afrag. Open leaguer was formed on 18th November. Guns and vehicles were kept ready to move, for it was hoped from day to day that the Division would be sent forward again. But as the days passed into weeks, and the weeks into months, Tmimi was developed into a residential estate.

## 2. Tmimi to Mareth

TMIMI WAS AS UNLIKE THE CONVENTIONAL DESERT as the Beau Geste version of dancing girls and Arabesque grandeur. There were sudden valleys fresh with the desert crocus and anemones and red poppies. The illusion was almost complete—one sometimes believed one could walk through heather and golden broom.

1st Armoured Division created a civilised oasis where a high standard of social and military life flourished for three months. No one in England, pitying the soldiers of the desert, could possibly have imagined the style in which Batteries celebrated Christmas, 1942. All manner of rare foods, even turkey, came up from the Delta or was miraculously discovered by Battery reconnaissance parties, and there were beer, spirits, wine—even angostura and Plymouth gin !

Liaison prospered with the armoured regiments. One result was that the cavalry began to learn the rudiments of field artillery work which later became so popular that indirect fire was almost an obsession—until tank encounters encouraged snap-shooting again.

Many parties were held with the various regiments, sports events, including competition for the Tmimi football cup, and training despite the rigorous petrol rationing which for weeks prevented the movement of any vehicles.

An interesting entry appears in the Regimental war diary for 23rd December, 1942. " The following message received : ' The Commander-in-Chief Mediterranean Fleet will be shooting at duck in the Bomba district. It is requested that all other sportsmen will refrain from shooting in this area. All informed ' ". Coyly you will observe, shooting *at* duck. This may seem on the surface the characteristic spirit of the period spent at Tmimi.

Yet these three months were not by any means wasted because they afforded a rest to the battle-weary members of the Brigade and the training undertaken on sand table and in mobile schemes was in no small measure responsible for successful subsequent operations. For several weeks nearly all the Regimental transport was engaged in convoying petrol from Tobruk to Benghazi. This enterprise was General Montgomery's improvisation when harbour installations in the port of Benghazi were wrecked by storms. The Division's " haulage company " helped the fighting forces to breach the Agheila line and crack on towards Tripoli.

Early in the Tmimi period Lt.-Col. R. W. Goodbody took over command of the Regiment from Lt.-Col. Leggatt, and Major D. Morris joined " E " Battery. Forthwith the new C.O. plunged into Battery and

Lt.-Col. R. W. Goodbody takes over command from
Lt.-Col. W. M. Leggatt, D.S.O., December 10th, 1942.

Regimental training to revive technical knowledge which, to be honest, had become dim as the natural consequence of the Regiment's rôle with 25-pounders in excessively close support of armour and the immediate change to an entirely different equipment with only six weeks pre-Alamein preparation.

The Regiment's future movements were uncertain but there was an almost permanent order to move regardless of the highly developed township which had been built of imposing marquees, wooden structures, interspersed with more humble canvas " woggeries." The Regiment had learnt to fend for itself so well through hard experience that no matter how poor the habitation everyone had a fireplace during these cold and wet days, and such refinements as toast for breakfast were not uncommon. Tripoli had already fallen when at last the Regiment's guns left Tmimi township on 21st February heading vaguely for a Divisional concentration area—" somewhere, perhaps, near Tripoli."

There would have been grave misgivings had the Regiment known it was to be ordered straight into the Mareth battle and carry on until the end of the Tunis campaign with vehicles which had taken such heavy punishment on the Tobruk-Benghazi run, some seven journeys apiece, 600 miles each way. Here was a classic illustration of the cheerful efficiency of drivers imbued with the principle " drive like hell—and when in trouble, ' Maaleesh, brew up.' " The durability of the vehicles proved how well their maintenance had been carried out no matter what strain was imposed night and day.

The guns left Tmimi on transporters. The remainder of the Regiment moved as a wheeled echelon, travelling just under 1,000 miles in a fortnight. In some parts the journey resembled an attractive holiday tour of North Africa but in others it was most unpleasant. The contrast is illustrated in the following two extracts from the war diary :—

7th March. " To-day we covered about 96 miles. We had a pleasant bathe."

9th March. " Off at 07.15 hours. Midday khamseen started and continued for the rest of the day. We pushed on and at 17.30 hours halted on 'A' track 7524. Covered about 107 miles. Unpleasant evening of violent dust storm. Passed hundreds of mines and had to leaguer on the track."

Just beyond Agedabia a relic of the Regiment's early misfortune was discovered, when the O.P. carrier " RC " lost by "A" Battery a year before was found on a dump of wrecked vehicles by the side of the road.

The column did not enter Tripoli but, slipping round, raced wildly along the road towards Mareth. From time to time the C.O. would pull up at the side of the road and, pumphandling his arm, urge every driver " to get the stick out." Wheels and tracks joined up again at Medinine. Here on 14th March the position was briefly : The enemy had made an unsuccessful armoured attack towards Medinine on the southern flank of the Mareth Line and lost 58 tanks, chiefly through the steady discipline and excellent shooting of the Guards Brigade. Prior to this attack Rommel had said, " If this fails the days of Afrika Korps are numbered." No one ever made a more accurate prediction.

The Regiment went into action among the olive groves near Medinine with O.P.s on a hill known locally as " Edinburgh Castle " (Point Optique). The Divisional artillery occupied positions around this area but there was very little action. The inaction was relieved one day by an extraordinary demonstration of armoured might when the cavalry cavorted in front of the hills held by the enemy and the Batteries joined in an enormous artillery concentration, which, we were credibly informed later by prisoners, wounded one Italian.

When the Mareth attack proper opened under the customary Eighth Army barrage, the infantry made very slow progress against strong-points, minefields and a network of interlocking defences. Contrary to the intelligence reports, the enemy had replaced inferior Italian troops with crack German troops and it was clear that success by a frontal attack would be achieved only at a too expensive cost. It was then that General Montgomery decided to switch the attack and put in an armoured left-hook along the route discovered by Popski's Private Army, followed by the New Zealand Corps.

## 3. The Left Hook

WITHOUT WARNING, ON 23RD MARCH, THE REGIMENT was ordered to move south through Foume Tatahouine. This was the beginning of the famous " left-hook " to Hamma directed upon the Gabes Gap in a wide encircling movement which outflanked the Mareth Line proper.

Slowly the guns moved back trying to leave the line unnoticed. But enemy O.P.s in the hills must have been astounded by hundreds of curling dust snakes streaming towards Medinine. Again, tanks and Priests were transported while wheels travelled in a separate convoy. After travelling all night and the following day the two columns rejoined at the road end and moved out across the desert. All that day until well into the night the Batteries churned their way without rest or pause save to fill up and snatch a quick brew. Off again at first light next day and after covering 300 miles of extremely sandy desert, leaguered behind the New Zealanders.

All this time not a single enemy aeroplane was seen and everyone imagined that Rommel had been deceived; an impression later discovered to be false. It was believed that the Division was upon Rommel's right flank unsuspected and that the armour would establish itself in the Gabes Gap before Rommel could extricate his main forces contained by the infantry in the Mareth Line.

As darkness fell on 25th March the Regiment leaguered for the last time in the desert proper. Henceforth it was to move either across moorlands or among the date and olive groves of cultivated areas. The location that night was roughly 20 miles south of El Hamma. The Batteries were not into leaguer complete until nearly midnight. Inert figures sprawled around the vehicles waiting for orders, what time drinking the gin and lime almost inevitably produced at these times. When the Battery Commanders returned from the Regimental " O " group they imparted the following plan : The New Zealanders, supported by 8th Armoured Brigade, were to attack the enemy's prepared position under a heavy barrage. Ground forces would be supported by the most concentrated aerial bombardment yet made, in which 15 squadrons of fighter-bombers, five squadrons of Spitfires and two squadrons of Hurricane tank-busters would co-operate. Then the final phase, " 1st Armoured Division will pass through the New Zealand Corps whether objectives have been gained or not; and break through to El Hamma."

It must be remembered that this happened in the early days of close support and co-operation by the Air Force with the Army and it seemed that this would be a blitzkreig *in excelsis*. After a short sleep before the attack the Batteries moved out to join their armoured regiments, and the three battle groups were ready soon after midday.

The whole plan was a brilliant success. It was the first time tanks had been launched in organised night-firing operations. The enemy were disrupted and, like their punch-drunk Mark IIIs. at Alamein, were unable to put up any effective resistance to this mighty cavalcade of armour.

The Brigade advanced in a solid phalanx lead by The Queen's Bays and 9th Lancers, one regiment on each side of the main road, while 10th Hussars were echeloned back to protect the Brigade transport.

The Batteries moved immediately behind their own regiments. First the columns negotiated a series of minefields along the familiar white-taped lanes and, liquidating a few anti-tank guns, penetrated two miles into the enemy lines before halting to wait for moonrise. Tank crews dismounted and the groups assembling to discuss the form were vividly reminiscent of the " eve of Waterloo " at Alamein. "All the trouble in my life," remarked one cavalryman, pointing at the rising moon, " has been caused by that leery old man, one way and another."

Enemy gun positions were still in action on all sides, firing overhead into the area of the bridgehead first torn by the New Zealanders and then exploited by the Brigade. At 01.30 hours the advance continued in so concentrated a form that the whole Brigade moved on a front of 200 yards astride the road. Lumbering along in the ghostly moonlight, the Shermans kept up continuous machine-gun fire. Burning vehicles and abandoned guns littered the route. Enemy infantry were flushed from hidden wadis; enemy guns captured and destroyed on both sides of the road. Two miles short of El Hamma an 88-millimetre anti-tank gun held up the advance for 15 minutes before it was destroyed. The Brigade was then ordered to halt till daylight. This was the beginning of the three-days' battle for El Hamma, southern bastion of the Gabes Gap.

*Crown Copyright reserved.*

**The 105 mm. gun-howitzer mounted in a " Priest."**

Enemy anti-tank guns, including 88-millimetres, were hidden in the palm trees. Self-propelled guns, tanks and heavy artillery, including 210-millimetres were moved round to delay the advance until forces in the Mareth Line could be withdrawn. The German gunners, veritable dervishes, raked the Brigade's area with fire. At one time the three Batteries were firing north-west, north-east, and south, for the Brigade, having broken through, sat isolated while elements of German armour and infantry formations swirled around the concentration.

Just after dawn on the first day, some 20 German tanks were reported approaching from the rear. Apparently they intended to bite off the echelons but they broke on the anti-tank gun screen and retreated from the spirited gallop by a squadron of 10th Hussars' tanks with " B " Battery guns in support. Meanwhile, the other two regiments with "A" and " E " Batteries had reined back upon meeting concentrated shellfire and close range anti-tank guns in the groves on the outskirts of El Hamma. It was in this engagement that Capt. Butler-Stoney and Lieut. Laskey were killed in the devastating 210-millimetre shellfire.

The enemy gunners continued airburst 88-millimetre shellfire during the night and among other targets hit the headquarter leaguer. The next morning a 210 concentration caught some of the guns but they were extricated without casualties. Capt. Drage and his crew were rescued under a smokescreen by a tank which towed their disabled Titanica from the sand dunes where it had become bogged on the left of The Bays' leading troop.

During these three days the lines of communication were secured, the divisional artillery concentrated around the Regiment and a full-scale shooting match was held. 7th Motor Brigade secured high ground on the right overlooking the plain stretching away towards Gabes. The enemy were routed and the Division took over 3,000 prisoners, with a bag of some 11 tanks and 81 guns, while the knocked-out vehicles were never counted.

The New Zealanders and 8th Armoured Brigade advanced through the hills behind 7th Motor Brigade and drove on towards Gabes. In the early morning of 30th March armoured cars of 12th Lancers stealthily drove forward through the palm trees and entered El Hamma. The Division was ordered to advance at mid-morning. Within an hour tanks, guns and echelons were off in full cry, sweeping through El Hamma and out on to the broad plain before Akarit. Here the enemy held a strong fortified line on the mountains running in a half moon from Djebel Roumana, almost on the sea, to a large salt lake. No matter how well sited in the wadis, positions on the plain were in full view of the enemy O.P.s in the mountains. Consequently everyone felt the enemy had an unhealthy advantage in the ensuing artillery duel, since the British guns were shooting blind at, and over, a bleak and impassive rock face.

The Army Commander decided to force this line with an infantry attack supported by the Desert Air Force and a heavy artillery barrage, and pass the armour through the gap. This was accomplished on 6th April. The extraordinary scenes that day were the nearest conceivable approach to a film battle. The British and Indian infantry were splendid. They advanced in open order across the plain to the foothills, utterly unmoved under the terrible shellfire which swathed their extended ranks. The Scots fought a terrific battle on Akarit at close quarters with the Germans, while the Indians slashed the Italians—literally—in the Fatnassa Hills. Prisoners poured down through the smoke shrouding the hillsides ; their winding columns eventually totalled 8,000.

Next day the Brigade formed up in regimental groups and at midday drove unopposed through the Tabaga Pass. The intention was to join up with the Americans thereby encircling the Afrika Korps. Armoured cars did in fact meet the Americans, but although American voices were picked up on the wireless nets, the Americans were not in the Mezzouna area when the Brigade arrived. Instead enemy tanks were encountered. Once again the three Batteries were firing all round the compass. That evening, the Bays and 10th Hussars, supported by "A" and "B" Batteries, carried out a sweep over the hills, closing in towards Mezzouna. The attack halted short of the village and the groups leaguered on one of the most bitterly cold nights of the entire African campaign.

On the following day Mezzouna was entered and the advance developed into a gallop 40 miles north. The enemy were then reported to be falling back beyond Sfax which was taken by 8th Armoured Brigade while the Regiment's guns were engaging armour some 12 miles inland on the right flank. When the Brigade had overcome this rearguard the whole force was ordered to a Divisional rest area, where the Batteries were gathered together around Regimental Headquarters at Bou Thadi to sit for two days eating broad beans, drinking red wine and being bombed at night with crackerjacks.

The Regiment turned in for maintenance and there were the usual rumours about the future, especially when it was rumoured that 1st Armoured Division would probably not take part in any further fighting in North Africa. This did not prove an accurate forecast by any means. The Regiment heard it was to leave the Eighth Army on loan to the First Army. 1st Armoured Division were indeed required later and the Regiment then rejoined the Division, but until the Tunis campaign ended the Regiment fought principally with 6th Armoured Division of First Army.

Tracks and vehicles once again divided into two columns and set out from Bou Thadi on a wide 300 miles circle through Sbeitla to join the First Army at Le Kef. The Regiment leaguered in a fragrant pine wood and rested for two days. Here the 11th Regiment for the first time met the 12th Regiment, who were also under command of 6th Armoured Division.

The Americans and First Army could not quite conceal their astonishment when meeting " desert rats " but nevertheless gave everybody an amiable welcome. First Army compo rations seemed too good to be true, particularly the English cigarettes instead of the " Vs " which had been the normal desert issue. Many First Army customs created surprise, most particularly the central feeding system employed even in the forward defence lines which seemed then, after so long on vehicle cooking, to be archaic. The vehicle brewcan had become the household god of troops in the desert; the surest way to distinguish an Eighth Army from a First Army vehicle was by the filthy, soot covered brew can dangling from the tailboard.

## 4. End in Africa

WITHIN A FEW DAYS THE 11TH WENT INTO ACTION alongside the 12th in direct support of 26th Armoured Brigade and as part of the artillery grouped under C.R.A., 6th Armoured Division. The assault was planned as an attack from Medjaz el Bab to Tunis, the first phase by infantry, followed by an armoured breakthrough. The Americans were to converge on Tunis from the direction of Bizerta, the French at Pont du Fahs and the Eighth Army at Enfidaville to contain the enemy on their fronts. 6th Armoured Division and 1st Armoured Division were to destroy enemy armour and cover the right flank of 5th Corps in the Medjez-Tunis attack.

The three Batteries were allocated one to each of three armoured regiments of the 26th Armoured Brigade, "A" to the 17th/21st Lancers, " B " to the 16th/5th Lancers and " E " to the Lothian and Border Horse. Batteries were to support the initial infantry attack with a concentration and then pass through behind the armour.

Reconnaissance parties were sent out to sight and survey a gun position where the guns could lie up under cover until they opened fire at zero hour. The Priests moved in by night along a tortuous mountain track and immediately ran into trouble. An enemy battalion had infiltrated throught the forward defence lines and " E " Battery found Germans installed on the crest in front of their gun position. Half an hour past midnight with the Battery still coming into action, one or two officers, walking forward about 100 yards in front of the gun position were greeted with a fusilade of rifle shots. Their reaction was immediate

—they whipped off their white sheepskin coats and retired. The firing increased and a party of infantry was located immediately in front of the guns. The Priests were reined back 200 yards to a wadi, gun control was ordered and they opened fire at 300 yards range with 105-millimetre and .5 Brownings. The enemy, discovered later to be paratroops, had by this time reached the ammunition dumps and one of the dumps was set ablaze. The guns kept up a shattering fire and the enemy fell back until by dawn the position was again secure. By this time, however, the infantry had been thrown back from the main hill feature in front, thus leaving the guns exposed in the forward defence lines. During the day the Battery was heavily engaged, but armour plating prevented casualties. Capt. McAllum shared the same ridge with the enemy's O.P. until towards evening when the infantry recaptured the feature and with it the enemy O.P.

This unforeseen adventure held up the entire plan of attack. When the attack did go in next day the Regiment fired concentrations in support of 46th Division. At mid-morning 26th Armoured Brigade swept through the attacking infantry towards the Goubellat Plain. Mines had been scattered heedlessly, sometimes in the middle of cornfields, and no minefields were marked. Several tanks were blown up including Lt.-Col. Goodbody's. Two of the crew were killed, but the C.O. escaped with only an injury to his leg. He could not be persuaded to go into hospital but went back to Divisional Headquarters whence, from time to time he came up to visit

**Gorge of Shabet el Acre, at Kerrata.**

the Regiment, where his place had been taken over by Major Richmond, who commanded the Regiment until the end of the campaign in Tunisia. Major Maclaren, who became second in command, was succeeded in "B" Battery by Major D. Rowlandson.

The advance proceeded slowly with the 17th/21st on the right and 16th/5th on the left. The Batteries dropped into action for short engagements against enemy tanks, self-propelled guns and 88s, and then pushed on again to catch up with the armour. The enemy fought courageously but were forced to surrender or retreat under the determined infantry close-quarter fighting and the movement of the British armour.

A heavy tank battle developed when the Brigade reached the Djebel Kournine, an enormous peak which dominated the whole plain. "A" Battery, behind the 17th/21st who were leading at this point, scored two direct hits on Mark VIs., which brewed up most successfully. The enemy relied principally upon mobile defence, using armour which included many Mark VIs. and Mark IVs., and for a short time, until the Royal Air Force intervened, used waves of fighter-bombers with a squadron of tank-busters. The enemy's forward troops were not exempt from the Luftwaffe's targets and suffered as much as the British. Possibly the Luftwaffe pilots were confused by clouds of smoke going up on both sides. The Regiment's contribution was to fire smoke anywhere within the enemy lines whenever the O.P.s spotted attacking planes. There is no doubt that by this time the Desert Air Force were infinitely better than the Luftwaffe, not only in providing fighter cover but in giving close support to ground troops.

Meanwhile, 1st Armoured Division advanced along the Goubellat Plain on the left of 6th Armoured Division. The Regiment was relieved by the 12th and ordered to rejoin 1st Armoured Division directed towards Azziz, another high feature. Mines were scattered everywhere by the retreating enemy. Approaching Azziz, 9th Lancers were forced to form their cruiser squadron into single file to negotiate difficult wadis. The enemy had hidden 88-millimetre anti-tank guns in cactus groves, with one of their guns covering this defile. The gunners held their fire until almost point-blank range and then opening up first on the rear tank, knocked out all eight tanks of the squadron in a row.

All that day the Luftwaffe made perpetual sorties to machine-gun and bomb the British lines, while the infantry battle on the left at Longstop rose to its crescendo. After shooting up several 88s and many infantry positions the armour rallied back and during the night the Regiment left with the tanks to relieve 6th Armoured Division, leaving an anti-tank gun screen on the plain.

6th Armoured Division had pushed forward under the very slopes of Kournine, and 1st Armoured Division took over for a most uncomfortable period. Enemy O.Ps. on Kournine had such perfect observation that they knew location of Divisional and Brigade Headquarters. How fortunate that they either lacked guns or ammunition to the extent that they had possessed at El Hamma. Nevertheless, the enemy gunners were very accurate and G.P.O.s did careful reconnaissances in order to work guns forward into wadis where at least they were hidden from direct observation. It was fortunate that the 105-millimetre charges were flashless since flashes would have revealed the gun positions, whereas the sound of firing only vaguely indicated the area.

Kournine itself was impregnable, honeycombed with passages and reinforced O.Ps. guarded by machine-gun nests and hundreds of booby traps. Successive infantry attacks were thrown back and it was realised that nothing short of a major offensive would penetrate the enemy lines between Kournine, the Argoub feature and Azziz.

The Batteries indulged in a riot of observed shooting, using " winkle " guns to snipe enemy tanks and also opened a cockshy at Kournine itself. Every half hour or so, throughout the 24 hours of the day, a dozen black puffs of airburst spattered the peak to keep the O.P.s restless, while the tanks raked the mountain sides with their 75-millimetre H.E.

The battle settled down into a static period which was very trying for everybody's nerves. But the Regiment obtained good results from its shooting as, for instance, in the two tank brews and the destruction of petrol and stores in a Regimental shoot by airburst indication, conducted by " B " Battery. The incentive in this case was perhaps sharpened by the presence of " The biggest niner this side of the Nile," who watched the shoot and whose presence and interest were reported by the C.O. in surreptitious warnings and adjurations over the Regimental net.

On 3rd May the Regiment was relieved for a short rest and, as one of the Battery Commanders remarked, " left Kournine with universal pleasure and unparalleled speed at 20.00 hours."

After another night march to 6th Armoured Division, five miles south of Medjez el Bab, Batteries joined their Regiments and pulled clear of the roads into hideouts in the woods for a day's rest. On 5th May, details arrived of the plan for the final drive on Tunis. It was to be an infantry attack with 7th Armoured Division passing through 4th Indian Division on the left of the Medjez-Tunis road, while 6th Armoured Division were to advance through 1st British Infantry Division on the right of the road. The Regiment was under command 26th Armoured Brigade which, with 201st Guards Brigade brought down from Eighth Army, composed 6th Armoured Division.

As dusk fell on 5th May, the Regiments moved out of their hiding places and concentrated in the field-gun areas. The infantry attack was in full swing by midnight and at dawn the objectives had been secured notwithstanding many isolated pockets left to be cleared up later. 26th Armoured Brigade passed through the white-taped lanes in the minefields and fanned out towards Bordj el Frendj. The armour was greeted with some shelling from the right flank and there was a most unpleasant encounter when the enemy tanks, wheeling away from the Brigade spearhead, darted in on the right. One of " B " Battery's O.P. tanks was knocked out by a Tiger, but 16th/5th Lancers in retaliation brewed this and another Tiger in quick succession.

All three Batteries and Regimental Headquarters were attacked from the air indiscriminately by both sides and finally "A" and " B " Batteries each had prematures. Everything considered, this was an unhappy and foreboding start, quite unlike the succession of brilliant achievements which followed.

The attack was never allowed to lose momentum. While 7th Armoured Division progressed swiftly on the left of the road, the Americans closed in along the coast. 26th Armoured Brigade were ordered to dominate Bordj el Frendj, where a cluster of farm buildings on the ridge surrounded by fields speckled with hay stooks made an almost English scene. Batteries had excellent shooting, principally against enemy anti-tank guns. Suddenly about 100 enemy interrupted " E " Battery's placid destruction. They appeared out of the ground around and about the guns—but they only wanted to surrender. They complained they were A.-A. gunners with not the slightest idea of how to fight tanks and, anyhow, half their battery had been drowned on the way over, while they had also lost most of their equipment. This was a typical illustration of the pessimistic outlook which characterised the enemy now being rounded up on all sides.

Dozens of 88-millimetres had been sited hastily on the top of the ground and, at Mornagnia on 7th May, " A " Battery accounted for six of them while " B " and " E " carried on similar work on each side, airbursting enemy infantry and anti-tank guns, and literally blasting a path for the leading tanks.

On 7th May, Derbyshire Yeomanry armoured cars penetrated into Tunis. 7th Armoured Division also entered the city on their front. The main force of 6th Armoured Division swung east away from Tunis, directed against the Cap Bon Peninsula, and the advance was unopposed until the outskirts of St. Germaine, a town of lovely seaside villas used by the Germans for Headquater offices and billets.

General Alexander's plan was to force the Hammam Lif gap, cut off the Cap Bon peninsula and bear down upon the enemy's rear in the Enfidaville position, while the Navy and Air Force prevented a Dunkirk from the beaches. Any student on the most improbable T.E.W.T. might have been excused the opinion that the task given to the 6th Armoured Division was quite impossible. They were set to capture St. Germaine and Hammam Lif, two towns in the narrow coastal plain which was only about three miles wide between the sea and the mountain range which rose abruptly to encircle the base of the peninsula. While 6th Armoured Division were driving through the Hammam Lif gap, 1st Armoured Division were to press through the mountains in the centre from Kournine and 4th Indian Division were ordered to scour the peninsula itself.

Anti-tank guns and huge mortars (nebelwerfers) opened up as the leading tanks of 26th Armoured Brigade approached St. Germaine. The intensity of the fire proved that this was the main enemy line and would be, undoubtedly, the last stand in the campaign. Heedless of the risk, and not without casualties, the tanks crept into St. Germaine accompanied by O.P.s, while the Batteries gave continual support. People of St. Germaine —and later of Hammam Lif—were quite openly wild with delight. They scattered flowers on the tanks and even climbed aboard while the guns were still firing. One old lady almost in tears stood at a street corner pouring out tea for anyone who had the time to stop, and she apologised because she had run out of her meagre milk and sugar rations.

It was here that the Regiment played one of the most astonishing games imaginable, namely, "hunting the Bey of Tunis." A message that the Bey had escaped in a blue car and must be stopped, which was sent over the wireless net, was variously interpreted until the Batteries were bringing in contributions of anyone from a westernised oriental gentleman's secretary wearing a blue suit in a cab drawn by a bay mare, to the Bey's private laundryman.

The 88-millimetre anti-tank guns and heavy 210-millimetres were keeping up constant opposition to the tanks. With unsurpassed courage 26th Armoured Brigade pushed on and on the night of 8th/9th May the Guards Brigade obtained a footing on the first hill above St. Germaine, overlooking the gap. On 9th May the German line was breached in a perilous undertaking, as one incident alone will prove—five tanks were knocked out in a row along one street, but happily the sixth, one of the Battery O.P.s, escaped undamaged. Over 30 anti-tank guns were located, although many were sited in A.-A. positions and others had been brought round and sited along the road in an endeavour to thicken the defence. Capt. Smith of "B" Battery, who worked forward on to Guards Hill, picked off four 88s on top of the ground bordering the road.

The final onslaught at Hammam Lif on 9th May was preceded by several heavy artillery concentrations on the town itself. The attack was made under a creeping barrage directed by Capt. Thomson-Glover of "E" Battery. This is his account of the engagement :—

"The Battery O.P. was moved forward into some olive groves to within 800 yards. The tanks slanted off to the left, troop by troop at wide intervals. At first three guns in front of the town held up the advance but they were neutralised sufficiently to allow the tanks to rush them. Our tanks kept extending and pushing on their left flank and we fired the whole Regiment, Batteries taking part in turn. The fire was controlled partly by observation and largely from reports by the tank commanders. In the close quarters of the town this was the only way to keep the fire just in front of the point tank without resorting to the preparation of a barrage.

"After two hours fighting the tanks had worked through the town. The other two armoured regiments rushed through and fanned out into the open country beyond.

"The local population cheered madly. The Bey's bodyguard turned out in fine fancy dress uniform to provide a ceremonial guard of honour, while in all this confusion our infantry with rifles at the high port cleared the town of all remaining enemy snipers. The Brigade captured Hammam Lif with the loss of only nine tanks, and bagged, jointly with us, as they kindly put it, nine 88s, five 50-millimetres, a battery of Bredas, and about 80 vehicles."

The evening was more peaceful. " E " Battery attempted to shell a ship lying off the Cap Bon peninsula and engaged scattered infantry on the hilltop with indirect fire. The Germans fired back indiscriminately and many of their shells fell harmlessly into the sea. By now the whole Brigade had galloped through the town bottleneck into the open country beyond. But there were still isolated enemy snipers about, some of whom engaged " B " Battery from houses along the beach. The gunners spattered these houses with their Brownings and parties of gunners—turned infantry—cleared the sand dunes and houses. Proof of this private battle was given to a sceptical Regimental Headquarters in a broadcast of battle noises over the rear link from the H truck, and a German prisoner was held ready to add his voice as further proof if the chatter of the guns could not finally convince the unbelievers.

Beyond Hammam Lif in the Grombalia area, where 6th Armoured Division were due to meet 1st Armoured Division, the Regiment split up for a couple of days to support the armoured regiments in independent columns. "A" Battery roared at a good 35 miles per hour through villages where street fighting was still in progress, heading straight for Hammamet on the coast. The German rout began in earnest. Thousands of prisoners threw down their arms and shambled along the roads. Guns and vehicles were abandoned, only a small proportion burnt. The Germans opposite the Eighth Army were cut off from retreat and it was clear that organised defence must soon end.

6th Armoured Division was ordered on to Bou Ficha, with " B " Battery's regimental group of 16th/5th Lancers leading. As the Battery approached Bou Ficha, tactical Headquarters of 1st Armoured Division was discovered in a hedgerow. General Briggs, commanding the Division, said that it was one of the happiest moments of his life when the Priests galloped out of the dust and the gunners waved him an hilarious greeting. The leading group was held up by anti-tank guns on the outskirts of Bou Ficha and also by a bridge blown under the C.O.'s wheels. Touring the countryside he and Lieut. Baker drove in an armoured O.P. car down the main road towards the bridge—which blew up as they braked, stopped, and hurriedly retired. The guns hammered Bou Ficha until tanks and infantry worked through the village during the night.

Next day the attack rolled on steadily until only six miles separated the two armies, the Eighth in the south at Enfidaville, and the First in the north. News was received that the Germans had offered surrender if they could be accorded the honours of war—and that the General had refused. Rumour had it that he had sent back a stiffish note saying that surrender would be accepted only under white flags—and if the enemy chose to ignore this suggestion, well then they could stay where they were and take what was coming to them. Laconically the note ended " Bombers are now on their way."

At 15.00 hours the Batteries were ordered to stop firing and remain silent unless ordered to fire by Regimental Headquarters. The guns were then the most forward of any in the Army. Leading tanks backed slowly to the cover of olive groves. The O.P.s waited on the forward fringe of the groves, looking over the silent and deserted plain which stretched from the sea on the left to the mountains about three miles away on the right. The main road ran straight ahead parallel with the sea, 300 yards from the beach. A few minutes after 15.00 hours a line of smoke shells marked the north boundary of the enemy's positions while Eighth Army gunners did the same in the south. The silence over the battlefield was broken only by the rhythmic sound of gunfire and the shells whistling over the olive groves to burst in plumes of spiralling white smoke.

Out over the sea echoed the throb of approaching planes and at 15.10 the first wave of 18 bombers in arrowhead came in steadily. German positions on the plain and in the foothills erupted under a fearful cascade of bombs. This happened three times at intervals of 10 minutes. At 15.30 the tanks with Besas spluttering galloped out of the silent olive groves. In a moment the enemy panicked. Tanks tore into their positions. Deserted wadis were suddenly thick with running figures. Trucks wheeled crazily in and out of the minefields. White flags fluttered everywhere in the enemy lines. The Afrika Korps had surrendered.

90th Light, the original desert enemies, kept up their morale to the end and marched in under their officers in ordered columns of threes, having destroyed all their equipment.

Some inconvenience was created when their commanders refused to surrender except to Eighth Army officers. Many prisoners spent that night with the Batteries, exchanging reminiscences of desert battles with the gunners. The Germans had recognised the divisional " rhino " signs and were able to give the gunners an account from the other side of the battles the two Divisions had fought.

The first man to complete the union of Eighth and First Armies was Capt. R. N. Smith, who drove along the coastal strip on the left of the road while 16th/5th Lancers' tanks charged forward.

The Eighth Army O.P. officers he met were a little chagrined to find that the men they had expected to be First Army were in fact Eighth Army. The group of eight officers who met on the blown bridge north of Enfidaville at 16.50 hours on 12th May, included seven O.P.s, of whom three were from " B " Battery—Major Rowlandson, Capt. Smith and myself. A few minutes later a Signals officer came down from the north and joined the group, hopefully expecting to drive on down the road as a short cut back to his unit with a load of beer he had obtained in Tunis. While the party on the blown bridge were having a ceremonial toast a column of enemy prisoners walked into an " S " minefield nearby and suffered horrible casualties. Lieut.-Col. J. A. T. Barstow (commanding 12th H.A.C.), appeared on the road in one of the 12th Regiment's O.P.s and he was standing with a group of 11th Regiment officers when the guns wheeled down the road to leaguer for the night.

The war in the desert was over. For several days the Regiment remained in the Bou Ficha area, bathing, celebrating, testing the German and Italian cars which almost everyone now ran. On one looting expedition Lieut. Baker rounded up some 300 Italians who had been overlooked in the hills.

Lieut.-Col. Goodbody returned and was able to attend a joint dinner of the 11th and 12th Regiments for officers and sergeants at Nabeul. This dinner was held in the evening of the victory march through Tunis in which the Regiment was represented by three officers—Major Richmond, Capt. Dudley Smith and myself—and 30 other ranks who marched on the right of 6th Armoured Division. Regimental Sergeant Major Butt carried out the duties of R.S.M. for 26th Armoured Brigade group.

Although this was the end in Africa it was soon evident that the war was by no means over, especially for the Regiment. Indeed, Mr. Churchill's words echoed forcefully : " This is the end of the beginning." A few days later the Regiment was ordered to join 51st (Highland) Division at Djedjelli.

# PART FOUR

## INVASION: MAY, 1943 — MAY, 1944

1. BOATING.

2. BATTLE OF SICILY.

3. ALGIERS INTERLUDE.

### 1. Boating

ON THE MORNING AFTER THE REGIMENTAL REUNION when, let it be confessed, there were many who, in signal terms, were not exactly on net, the Regiment pulled out of its Bou Ficha leaguer and in two columns headed for Djedjelli. The wheeled convoy arrived four days later while the tracks making a wide detour because of weak bridges, were eventually stopped by Movement Control near Constantine since the bridges ahead were said to be unsafe. As a matter of fact two Priests later successfully completed the route. When the Priests reached a bridge, the No. 1 popped out, had a look at the foundations and said, "I think this will be all right."

While the tracks waited disposal instructions from Movement Control, orders came from Regimental Headquarters to divert Priests and O.P. tanks to the Le Kroub workshops for overhaul and renewal. There, through the keenness and hard work of Lt.-Col. F. Hodges and his R.E.M.E. staff, who frequently worked night shifts, the somewhat worn equipment was renewed and many useful modifications (tank turret removals, etc.) were made according to the Regiment's specifications.

At Djedjelli the Regiment liaised with the Highland Division, carried out drill orders with skeleton equipment and feverishly practised boating drill. It was clear that the Regiment was going to join in the invasion of Europe, but the exact location of the invasion beaches was a secret from the troops taking part until they were actually in the L.C.T.s heading for Sicily.

During one of the training schemes, on 15th June, "A" Battery and a party of Regimental Headquarters were shipwrecked. This is a description of the wreck given at the time :—

"Our L.C.T. stuck firmly on the sandbank and drifted sideways on to the breakers. All attempts to move either under her own power or by shifting the vehicles around proved hopeless. The waves continued breaking over the ship filling the hold faster than the pumps could pump the water out, and the Colonel ordered all troops to be got ashore with rations, water and bedding.

"A hoist was improvised, but this was very slow and few people were successful in making a dry landing. The majority swam ashore and a chain was formed to pass the clothes and rations. The current was very fierce. Both the C.O.'s and B.C.'s batmen were in difficulties, but apart from a few cuts and bruises no one was really injured.

" Fires for cookhouses were started on the beach while the rescue work continued. The breeches buoy broke twice but by 21.00 hours all were ashore. The beach looked like the scene of a film shipwreck. Every man had a hot meal and tea, then the rain started to pour down and continued throughout the night.

" Fires were lit in the morning and drying out started. Again a chain was started to get the equipment ashore. An American fighter circled overhead and finally dropped a message from the second in command saying it was impossible to reach us by land and suggested marching. The Battery formed up in a single file carrying haversacks and water bottles. The C.O., on account of his recent wound, was unable to march and was left with the Acting Adjutant and the baggage party on the beach.

" The men of the Battery will long remember that march, which was led by an Arab guide. It was necessary time and again to climb up 1,000 feet on one hill, descend to the valley and up again. We did not reach the plain until 17.00 hours. There, to everyone's delight, was a farm kept by some charming French people who gave us tomatoes and fruit and sold us wine and lemonade. We telephoned our map reference to the Town Major and gave him a message for the Regiment. At 18.00 hours we began to march the eight kilometres to the main road but after five minutes we were met by the second in command with a fleet of small cars which ran a shuttle service to a ferry. Hot tea and rations were produced, and beyond the ferry a convoy of three-tonners stood ready to take us back to the camp.

" The men throughout the two days never made a single murmur or grumble. Many of them had worked in difficult positions in the water for as long as four hours at a time."

Towards the end of June equipment arrived with a rush to war establishment. The Regiment divided into the various embarkation groups at the beginning of July. Certain serials concentrated in Malta where General Montgomery made some very charming remarks about the Regiment.

## 2. The Battle of Sicily

THE REGIMENT'S GUNS were the first artillery to land in the invasion of Europe.

After a disagreeable voyage in a heavy sea the assault craft landed infantry and guns before dawn on 10th July at Pachino, on the southern tip of Sicily near Porto Paulo. All the guns and vehicles got ashore safely, although some had to waddle through five feet of water. Only one Priest lost its waterproofing and even this one came safely through, although the sea covered the piece. The Italians were demoralised by the rocket-firing ships, naval bombardment, aerial bombardment, infantry invasion and the mass of heavy equipment brought ashore on the first day. The Regimental party was scattered over a considerable area but all managed to concentrate within the first day.

The landing as far as the Regiment was concerned was practically unopposed. Instead of digging in under heavy shellfire, as had been imagined, everyone brewed-up in the morning sunshine, eating grapes gathered in the vineyards a mile or so inshore. On the first day only two ranging rounds were fired. The Royal Air Force controlled the air by day, but on the night of Day 1 and on successive nights the beaches were heavily bombed by the Luftwaffe.

The various serials landed from many different ships, but, having joined in a Regimental group it was possible to support the general advance of armour which went ahead much more swiftly than had been anticipated. The Priests resumed their normal armoured rôle and joined 50th Royal Tank Regiment on an axis of advance northwards through Noto towards Palazzolo. Here the enemy put up a strong fight, but his guns and mortars were eventually silenced. Resistance ceased appropriately at lunchtime and 1,400 Italians surrendered. Palazzolo township was very unpleasant, having been bombed into ruins by the air force. Through Palazzolo, on to Bucheri and up to Vizzini where, for the first time, the advance was seriously checked; the town Vizzini and surrounding heights were held in strength by the Herman Goering Reconnaissance Unit.

The whole of this advance had been carried out with a ridiculously small amount of transport. The infantry had to walk everywhere unless they could arrange an occasional ferry service on tanks. They produced many ingenious substitutes for baggage transport, pressing mules and donkey carts into service. The advance was pinned before Vizzini. During the fighting " B " Battery lost their Battery Commander, Major Rowlandson, when an airburst shell exploded near his tank. He was succeeded by Major J. P. Charles.

General alarm was raised when an enemy self-propelled gun—in reality going spare—appeared between the guns and the echelon and shot up a medium battery before it was silenced.

When the Highland Division came up they tumbled the enemy out of Vizzini. Vehicles, guns and many prisoners were left behind. Paratroops were used by both sides. There were constant paratroop infiltration scares and several German parachutists were captured in the Battery areas, fortunately before they could do any harm. From Vizzini the Batteries wound their way upwards through Militello, Francofonte and Scordia. The enemy fought rearguards in small and courageous pockets. There was perpetual danger from sniping in the orange groves and several tanks were knocked out by stalking German infantry besides anti-tank guns. M.E. 109s flew over on repeated strafing sorties, aided on 17th July by a squadron of Lightnings. " E " Battery suffered several casualties from M. E. raiders and later lost Capt. McAllum and his crew when their tank was set on fire. The enemy fell back slowly behind demolitions to the main defensive line which ran from Catania on the coast through the hills south of Mount Etna.

For some days the top of Mount Etna had been the main landmark. Forcing the Catania line the Regiment fought for about a fortnight underneath the mountain. Smoke from the steaming volcano curled across the horizon in pink and golden ribbons at sunrise and in the evening sunset. The enemy's positions were based on the river line west of Catania and included Gerbini, Sferro, Catenanuova, Centuripe, Regalbuto and Misterbianco. Support was given to attacks by Highland Division infantry on the Gerbini aerodrome and when the aerodrome was taken—littered with smashed equipment and aeroplanes—Capt. Page, of " B " Battery, found a crate of Leica telescopic cameras.

On the right, 50th Division were held up at Catania by almost impregnable defences which depended upon successive lines of trenches interlaced with barbed wire, pillboxes and minefields. The Canadians were on the immediate left, with the Americans on the west coast. Day after day the

Highland infantry tapped at the enemy's lines. Armour was unsuitable in this country of narrow, rock-walled roads. Since the Regiment were now Army troops, the guns were whisked from one front to another to support attacks with concentrations by night and observed shooting by day. The weather was abominably hot and the air vibrated in the sirocco until the afternoons were almost unbearable; and there was never the cool relief of evening in the desert. Fortunately, the orchards were heavy with oranges, almonds and grapes, and there were also many good wells as a change from the water in vehicle cans which by mid-morning was too hot to drink. A central maintenance and rest camp was established near Ramacca whence the Batteries sallied out to support attacks in different sectors, returning to the shade of almond orchards when the job was finished.

On 24th July the Regiment went out to support the Canadian attack around Catenanuova. The enemy had registered the winding mountain road and shellfire caused casulties to both Regimental Headquarters and " E " Battery. The enemy had excellent observation over the whole of the British lines. Priests were moved in the dark to whatever covered positions could be found. In this action the Regiment put down an airburst barrage, the first of its type in this war, registered by " E " Battery's O.P. on the top of Mount Scalpello. The airburst shells were superimposed on the H.E., fired by field and medium guns, and the infantry were delighted with the success of the barrage.

Finally, the infantry broke through at this point, with 78th Division from the North African First Army leading a superb attack to scale the heights of the mountain fortress at Centuripe. By this time the Priests were almost worn out and Batteries were having constant mechanical trouble. " B " and " E " Batteries, with Regimental Headquarters, therefore, decided to go into a rest area while "A" Battery continued the battle for a few days, first with the Canadians and then 78th Division, when theirs were the only guns able to put down a barrage for the attack on Adrano.

After Adrano had been taken, the advance continued to Bronte, and all vehicles had difficulties on the lava slopes of Etna. The Priests again proved themselves, ground their way through walls and over lava terraces into positions resembling the slag heaps of a gas, light and coke company. On 12th August "A" Battery supported the 78th Divisional attack on Maletto, then returned to the Regimental area near Regalbuto, by now completely deserted as the advance had rolled forward. Major Chrimes left the Battery, which was taken over by Major Dudley Smith. Capt. Drage was appointed Adjutant soon afterwards when Capt. Wathen left for hospital.

The Regiment moved to a pleasant place overlooking the sea near Catania. Current information was of a probale return to 1st Armoured Division in North Africa. Nevertheless the Regiment was not completely left out of the invasion of Italy cross the Messina straights. Most of the equipment had been withdrawn, or was in the process of being handed over, and the Regiment was reduced to using captured enemy guns. " E " Battery, led by Major D. Morris, worked day and night shifts to calibrate and then move two 12-inch howitzers, British-design Italian-made during the Great War. It was hoped to transport these enormous pieces to Messina, three tank transporters to a gun, but the pioneers of the " Heavy Artillery Company " were unceremoniously ordered off the road which their lumbering artillery had blocked. Undaunted, Major Morris went on to Messina where, with the help of Italian gunfitters in an Italian workshop, he put together an Italian 149-millimetre gun. This was calibrated and brought into action among American guns lined up for the barrage. After the Diesel tractor had crashed on a slope the gun was winched behind two quads on to a platform in the front garden of a house.

On the morning of 3rd September " E " Battery fired 76 rounds in three and a half hours at various concentration areas in Italy. Resistance within range soon ceased with the Italian collapse and the Battery was relieved—thoughtfully handing back their gun on signature to the Italian workshop.

Regimental life quickly developed into a quasi-peacetime routine. Two excellent Regimental dinners were held, first to the C.O., and the second to Brigadier John Currie, Brigadier Fellowes and Lt.-Col. Tom Smith. At this period the Regiment was under command 4th Armoured Brigade and before saying good-bye took part in a review organised upon the possibility of a visit by General Montgomery. Four complete regiments of Sherman tanks, plus armoured cars and guns, were formed up in review order. Once again the Regiment paraded on the right and were inspected first, an R.H.A. privilege gratefully acknowledged in that blistering heat.

## 3. Algiers Interlude

IN THE FIRST FORTNIGHT OF SEPTEMBER practically all equipment was handed over and what few belongings remained crated for shipment to North Africa. Using borrowed transport, the Batteries motored down to Syracuse and after an uncomfortable two days, uncertainly spent in inhospitable fields, boarded H.M.T. "Marigot," a small French cargo passenger boat. The Marigot steamed slowly into the Mediterranean and there anchored off Valetta for two days, where the surrendering Italian Navy was seen disporting itself in complicated manœuvres. The Italian motor torpedo boats were quite impressive. The C.O. sent a greetings signal to Viscount Gort, V.C., Governor General of Malta, who had recently been appointed Colonel-Commandant of the H.A.C. Lord Gort signalled back, but no one was allowed to go ashore and he was unable to visit the Regiment afloat.

When the " Marigot " came alongside the docks at Bizerta there were queries of " Just out from Blighty ? " from soldiers working on the dockside, who received a curt reply from gunners hanging over the rails— merely the Arabic " Aiwa."

The Regiment camped among old friends near Bizerta, where 2nd and 4th Regiments, R.H.A., produced a magnificent welcome. It was a timely arrival, for everyone was able to join in farewells to Brigadier " Friz " Fowler, who had been C.R.A. of 1st Armoured Division so long and so forcefully. A fortnight later baggage was once more packed up and the Regiment entrained to rejoin 1st Armoured Division in a pleasant concentration area among the farms inland from Algiers. All ranks were delighted to be " home " again. They took possession of six French farms and promptly organised them into comfortable billets, with the protection of roofs against the heavy autumnal and winter rain. At first only individual training was attempted since no Priests and controlled stores were released. Sand tables, discussions and classes were started at Regimental Headquarters and within the Batteries.

Early in December eight Priests were released with sufficient equipment for a Battery. " B " Battery took over the issue first and began a firing camp in the hills near Bir Rabalou. The other two Batteries went down in turn but the weather turned excessively cold and some of the training was ruined by heavy rain.

The Regiment was home again in its billets in the Maison Carrée-Sidi Moussa area for Christmas. The countryside was comparatively rich in local produce. Although American competition was keen, Regimental Headquarters and the Batteries were able to provide turkeys, poultry, pigs, vegetables and unlimited wine for superb Christmas festivities. Families at home were astonished to read letters in which they were told that champagne was on sale in the Battery canteens.

Early in the new year 2nd Armoured Brigade moved to a training area near Bouira and subsequently to Sidi Aissa. Again training was hampered by rain, especially at Bouira, where the camp area was churned up into mud 18 inches deep. Towards the end of this period Lt.-Col. Goodbody left the Regiment to command 2nd Armoured Brigade and soon afterwards sailed for liason work in the Anzio beachhead.

Lt.-Col. J. H. Slade-Powell succeeded him after a short interval. The Regiment began to receive more equipment, including new Priests, half-tracks, wireless and specialist equipment and later Khaki drill. What time life in 2nd Armoured Brigade had resumed the customary round of training, liaison and fond imaginings. 2nd R.H.A. had left with 43rd Lorried Infantry Brigade before Christmas for Italy. There were contradictory rumours regarding the Regiment's future, with opinions still divided between England for the Western Invasion, Italy, and even the Balkans.

Games and sports culminated in the defeat of Regimental Headquarters by "A" Battery on Christmas Day, 1943, when "A" Battery won for the second time the Tmimi Cup, and by the victory of "B" Troop, who won the Sidi Moussa Cup for sports at the Regimental gymkhana held in May. Large scale leave was then introduced and during one period half the Batteries went away at a time to a rest camp at Surcouf. Orders to mobilise once more were received in the middle of the month. Comfortable billets were vacated, not without regret yet with an enthusiasm for the anticipated renewal of active service.

The Divisional Royal Artillery group concentrated at "Z" Reception Camp, Cap Matafou, prior to embarkation for Italy. Priests and transport went by merchant ships and personnel embarked in the H.M.T. "Ville D'Oran" on the 22nd May.

★ ★ ★

# PART FIVE

## VICTORY : JUNE, 1944 — MAY, 1945

1. GOTHIC LINE.

2. CONQUEST IN ITALY.

## 1. Gothic Line

ALTHOUGH THIS WAS A RETURN TO CENTRAL MEDITERRANEAN FORCES, it was with a "new boy" feeling that the Regiment disembarked at Taranto towards the end of May. Some of the transport had arrived beforehand and was waiting at the dockside to carry baggage, but the men had to march to the transit camps. The feeling of shy loneliness was dissipated when officers of 4th Hussars on the quayside explained that they were running the transit camps. The 4th were very hospitable and on the first night gave a party which was a signal welcome to Italy. Fatigue parties were sent to help unload stores and later the Priests and M.T. During the voyage many items of equipment were damaged and lost, as were private possessions, and a Court of Enquiry later assembled to deal with the matter.

Major Richmond had gone over to Italy ahead, and the reconnaissance party of Battery Captains forgathered with him in a disused P.O.W. camp near Gravina. The Regiment followed but stayed in the large barn-like buildings of the P.O.W. camp for only a few days before moving out to a bleak hillside above Gravina, aptly called "Dartmoor" camp. The armoured regiments concentrated about 20 miles away. The Bays and 9th Lancers did a number of schemes to practise tank co-operation with infantry, while 10th Hussars moved to the Rome area for exercises with real infantry. Batteries sent representatives to join in the training of the regiments to which they were affiliated and themselves embarked on a programme of gunner training. In one of the schemes there was a regrettable accident when a shell bursting near a body of spectators wounded Brigadier Goodbody and killed his driver.

Great trouble was taken to experiment and compile range tables for the smoke shells, calibrate the Priests and complete their modifications. All this because it was hoped soon to resume a fighting rôle. Imagine, therefore, the disappointment when first transport and drivers were taken away to operate an M.T. delivery column and second, the Regiment was ordered back to the south to run transit camps. The administration of three transit camps occupied the majority of the personnel and the remainder set up a rest camp on the seashore near Taranto. The camp organisation was known as Harrods. The Regiment was responsible for three camps, Alexander, Dowler and Clarke. Harrods dealt with units going back to the Middle East for a rest and with French and American forces concentrating for the invasion of southern France.

The news of the western invasion, which was received at Gravina, although creating excitement had also made the Regiment feel a little despondent, and the sight of the Free French embarking for another invasion only added to the disappointment. The French forces were naturally very gay and elated at the prospect of liberating their own country, and there was an historic farewell on the quayside when the Regiment provided a guard of honour for the embarkation of General de Tessigny.

While the Regiment was thus split up and engaged not only in transit camps but in " Q " movement work at Brindisi, the blow that had long been feared fell without warning. A signal was received in July ordering Priests to be handed in and 24 Sextons to be drawn instead—the Sexton being a Canadian version mounting the 25-pounder gun. Protests were unavailing, although so much work had been put in compiling range tables and modifying the new Priests ready for action. Capt. R. Thomson, the new Technical Adjutant, and his staff handed over the Priests at Molfretta and within a few days had drawn a full complement of Sextons.

The Brigade was ordered to move north to a concentration area near Porto Civitanova. On the way the Sextons were halted to be fired for the first time when comparative calibration was carried out at Pedaso. Trouble was experienced with the all-metal tracks and a great panic was caused when all the spare track pins were used in a few days. It was then resolved to change the track for the rubber type as soon as possible.

After a few days near Civitanova it was clear that another battle was imminent. There was the usual checking up of equipment, ammunition scales, petrol, echelons, etc., and then the Regiment set out once more in two convoys to the 1st Armoured Division's concentration area near Iesi. The terrain was very different from any encountered previously, for the Sextons had to negotiate narrow tracks and the steep ascents of the Apennines. During this march rubber tracks were ferried forward and half the Sextons were changed over.

Once again there had been an eleventh hour rush to concentrate armour ready for a breakthrough. The plan was to assault the Gothic Line with infantry and pass 1st Armoured Division through 46th Division, directed upon Cesena and the north. The Brigade arrived in the line tired and sleepless after a journey of nearly a week, and on 3rd September were ordered to pass through. Just before setting off, an Air O.P. pilot arrived at Regimental Headquarters. He arranged to fly forward next morning and take pot luck about landing in whatever area the Regiment had reached.

After an all-night march along the tortuous tracks the Brigade crossed the River Conca near Morciano. The enemy defences were, however, far from broken and instead of a breakthrough the British tanks had penetrated only the outer defences of the Gothic Line. Towering heights—Montescudo, Gemmamo, Monte Colombo and the " neutral " state of San Marino—on the flanks and in front were still held by the enemy.

Manœuvre was restricted to a narrow front and the tanks had not penetrated very far beyond the Conca when they were halted by accurate and heavy shellfire, nebelwerfers and anti-tank guns. Batteries deployed into independent positions when the first cries for action were heard on the nets. By midday they had been collected into a Regimental area inside the bridgehead. In the afternoon a full-scale attack was laid on, The Bays and 10th Hassars leading under an artillery fire plan. Mines abounded everywhere and several tanks were lost.

As the tanks wheeled up to the start line there was preliminary evidence that this was going to be a sticky operation for they were sniped by enemy infantry concealed in the vineyards and ditches. German infantry knocked out several Sherman tanks with bazookas fired from hiding places in the ditches. Many bazooka-men were shot by tanks covering one another but it was extremely difficult to spot isolated men before they had fired. The Bays' tanks had a disconcerting experience when a bridge was blown some distance behind their leading squadron.

The momentum of the attack decreased and, far from reaching Coriano as had been planned for that morning, the Brigade had to fight its way to establish positions near San Clemente. The German artillery harassed gun positions and concentrations fell in the leaguers. From their O.P.s it must have been quite plain that Brigade Headquarters had been established near St. Clemente and that Divisional Headquarters, with a whole mass of echelons, was a little farther back to the rear. Accurate fire was directed upon these targets. At night single German aeroplanes in relays flew over and dropped " crackerjack " anti-personnel bombs, though there was no sign of the Luftwaffe by day. On the other hand the Desert Air Force sent over continual fighter-bomber raids to attack the German defences on the Coriano-Passano ridge.

All three regiments in turn, helped by the Batteries, attempted to support the infantry on to this ridge and eventually the Sherwood Foresters secured San Savino on the left, with 9th Lancers in support, after much hard fighting by Gurkhas of the 43rd Lorried Infantry Brigade.

The experiences of each Battery were much the same. Their O.P.s went forward in Sherman tanks and, under perpetual sniping and very heavy nebelwerfer " stonks," directed supporting fire. The volume of artillery support had increased beyond anything known in the Regiment's previous fighting. In the desert a regimental target had been something of a feat. Now O.P.s were calling for regimental targets as frequently as they had hitherto demanded Battery targets, and not infrequently calling for Divisional concentrations.

As the drill for shooting the Divisional artillery and medium guns of A.G.R.A. became more familiar, devastating fire support was obtained and whole areas neutralised within an average of five minutes from the O.P.s call for an " Uncle " target. The Air O.P. conducted many exciting shoots and proved very efficient at spotting targets such as anti-tank guns and tanks where locations were suspected but could not be verified by the ground O.P.s.

From the heights on the left the Germans mounted a counter-attack parallel with the River Conca. 9th Lancers deployed to help The Buffs holding Croce. A fierce engagement lasted all day and was renewed at night, but The Buffs held tenaciously and the danger was finally removed by operations by 56th Division and 46th Division which cleared the commanding features.

During the Croce battle the Regiment fired continually all afternoon and again in the barrage and D.F.s called for during the night. The " U " target drill was now in full swing and Major Morris controlled no fewer than seven regiments firing at the German infantry and tanks. The Air O.P. was also sent up and, working through a very enlarged regimental forward control direct to the medium regiment, materially helped to beat off the counter-attack which the Germans had mounted against this flank. Batteries were leapfrogged forward to support the advance, which was maintained despite many casualties to armour and infantry. Hundreds of German prisoners were taken in the repeated attacks. The Gurkhas were most handy with their kukris ! The volume of shellfire from tanks and guns, plus the relentless fighter-bomber attacks by the Desert Air

Force, gradually wore down resistance and created great carnage amongst the German troops.

From the Coriano-San Savino ridge the Gurkhas advanced to capture the Ripabianca ridge under a heavy barrage in which the Regiment participated. "B" Battery O.P.s provided close support to 10th Hussars, who were supporting the Gurkhas for this operation. Infantry pressed on and established a bridgehead over the River Marano near Ospedelleto. The Brigade crossed into the bridgehead and at exactly this time the weather broke in heavy rainstorms which converted all the tracks into lanes of mud and the fields into treacherous bogs. Orders were received that a vigorous attack must be made in an attempt to cut clean through the enemy lines. The Bays with 1st King's Royal Rifle Corps were given the task of capturing the commanding ridge known as Point 153, south of San Ermete and just beyond the northern tip of San Marino.

The attack was postponed that evening until dawn next day. When the tanks approached the start line in the early morning it was found that German infantry had infiltrated back into the houses. The King's Royal Rifle Corps were therefore called upon to secure this line and the main attack again postponed. By this time tanks of another formation had moved away from a ridge on the left and German tanks worked round in that direction and obtained positions from which they covered the approach to the start line. The Bays, supported by "A" Battery's O.P.s, pushed two squadrons forward under the lee of a sharp ridge beneath a track which ran through the houses the King's Royal Rifle Corps had cleared. Beyond this ridge the country fell away in many transverse wadis to a basin which rose again on the other side to the objective. At midmorning the attack was pressed under heavy artillery bombardment in which the Regiment assisted with H.E. concentrations and smoke. The Bays' tanks went over the ridge and down the other side into the wadis, where they were trapped by enfilade fire from three sides as anti-tank guns, Tiger tanks and S.P.s opened up at a few hundred yards range.

Crews baled out of tanks which were hit. They were machine-gunned and sniped by enemy infantry on all sides. Capt Drage, the "A" Battery F.O.O., and all his crew were killed. Capt Drage had rejoined the Battery from Adjutant three months earlier. The Bays lost 24 tanks. Meanwhile the whole divisional artillery was engaged in a repeat of the fire plan. A further attempt to blind the enemy was made by firing a heavy smoke screen and after the Regiment had used all its smoke neighbouring regiments took over the task until, in just under the hour, nearly all the smoke in the Divisonal first line had been expended. The infantry attacked again that night, cleared the feature and the Gurkhas crossed the next obstacle, the River Marecchia.

While the "A" Battery O.P.s were supporting 1st King's Royal Rifle Corps, who had been sent into the bridgehead with the Gurkhas, "B" Battery's O.P.s pushed forward with 10th Hussars to exploit the crossing.

Unexpected news was received that 1st Armoured Division was to be disbanded owing to lack of reinforcements. It was a distressing decision, especially for those who had served in the Division since the early days, but there was one comfort in that 2nd Armoured Brigade was preserved intact. Henceforward the general policy was to use 2nd Armoured Brigade as an independent brigade attached to an infantry division. The Regiment moved with the armour to give immediate support required and for all other gunner matters fell under Headquarters Royal Artillery of the Division with which the Brigade was working. Consequently, during the next few weeks the Regiment supported 46th, 4th and 56th British Infantry Divisions, moving slowly forward in the foothills as the attack gradually progressed through the Gothic Line towards Route 9 and the valley of the Po.

Daily rain storms drenched the countryside and ruined the mountain tracks so that movement, especially of tanks, was restricted on the narrow mud-coated lanes along which the divisions had to be supplied. River obstacles were met, to be crossed one after another first by the infantry, and then, when Sappers had performed their almost daily miracle of Bailey bridge building, by tanks and guns. Santarchangelo was taken, the Rubicon crossed, Savignano cleared and the advance continued beyond Montalbano, over the Fiumecino to Cesena. For every one of these operations there were many other minor attacks. Heavy barrages were fired so that the Regiment often shot 500 rounds per gun in one operation. The gunners had very little rest and were often soaked to the skin during all-night programmes.

Near Cesena the three Batteries occupied positions behind a crest which was at first not held by the infantry, and Batteries, therefore, sent out their own patrols. " B " Battery's O.P.s were concerned in harassing exploits near the Monastery until the enemy drew back once more and the nebelwerfer range receded. Route 9 had now been reached and, after crossing the Savio, the King's Royal Rifle Corps with "A" Battery in support were sent post-haste along the main road to capture Forlimpopoli.

" C " Troop guns firing barrage for the New Zealanders' attack on Celle, from S.E. of Faenza.

Capt. Baker was given a very friendly welcome when he entered the town by jeep. The Regiment raced up and again occupied positions where the Batteries produced their own local defence. The King's Royal Rifle Corps having captured the town, raced through to seize a crossing over the river Ronco.

A bridgehead was gained that night and Capt. Henderson went over as F.O.O. At first light enemy S.P.s counter-attacked with strong forces of infantry. These infantry were engaged by the Kings Royal Rifle Corps riflemen, but the S.P.s began shooting down the houses at point blank range. The position became untenable and the riflemen were ordered back across the Ronco. When they reached the bank they found the river had risen to a swirling torrent during the night and only the very strongest swimmers could possibly withstand the current. Enemy infantry infiltrated into the bridgehead and close-quarter fighting was going on in the shattered houses and in the fields. Capt Henderson stayed behind in a house with the Company Commander to attend to the wounded and they carried one man to the river bank. There they were engaged by a spandau. Capt Henderson shot one of the machine gunners and later he and the Company Commander swam the swollen river to safety.

Hand-to-hand fighting increased in the bridgehead and one or two unfortunate Riflemen who tried to swim the river were carried away by the current. Gunner Hirst, the F.O.O.'s signaller, was wounded and taken prisoner, but not before he had smashed his wireless set. The Riflemen cut off by the swollen river were lost.

A few days after this debacle, the Regiment was taken out for a short rest in the Bertinoro area. First " E," then the other two Batteries, went into action again to support the attack by 46th Division on the aerodrome and then on Forli town. While the Regiment was in positions at St.

**Ruts caused by ammunition half-tracks across battery position S.E. of Faenza.**

Martino in Strada the first allocation of leave to United Kingdom under the L.I.A.P. scheme was received and a party of one officer and twelve other ranks left on November 14th.

The enemy continued to fight delaying actions on the lines of the successive rivers and the Regiment supported the armour in the arduous fighting to secure bridgeheads over the Montone and Lamone, the Cosina canal and on to the Senio, in the course of which Faenza was first by-passed and then captured. The King's Royal Rifle Corps reappeared to make a brilliant attack which captured Marzeno,˙and preparations were then made for the major operation of crossing the Lamone. When the attack was made the infantry penetrated some 2,000 yards or more to secure the Pideura ridge, upon which the village of Pideura was the dominating point on the left, and at the other end the feature fell away to Celle, an enemy stronghold. This proved a most difficult operation, particularly in the supplying of forward troops over the winding, muddy tracks. The Regiment's O.P.s were cut off for four days under intense mortar and artillery fire on this ridge. Ultimately, all forward troops were supplied by mule and jeep trains from a central point which was built up inside the bridgehead. The situation was eased when the New Zealanders eventually captured Celle under a terrific barrage. The countryside resembled a conventional impression of the 1914-18 battlefield.

"A" Battery experienced a distressing period at this time. First Capt. Baker was gravely wounded, then, during counter-battery fire, a shell which hit "B" Troop command post killed the new Troop Commander, Capt. A. W. Grant, and Sgt. Smith, the Battery's popular and most efficient "Tiffy Sergeant."

The Gurkhas and New Zealanders secured Faenza and the Regiment moved to positions about two miles north of the town to celebrate the fourth Christmas abroad, fortunately in the warmth and comparative comfort of farmsteads.

"B" Battery were committed with 10th Hussars in support of 56th Division for a short time as the battle progressed towards the Senio, but early in the New Year the Regiment concentrated complete in a Brigade rest area at Pesaro. Persistent rain and snowstorms had turned the forward areas into seas of sticky mud and everyone was thankful to spend January in houses.

During January several squadrons of the armoured regiments were put into the line facing the Senio near Villanova; for the most part as dismounted infantry retaining one troop per squadron in tanks. They lived in uncomfortable conditions yet cheerfully performed unaccustomed duties, patrolling with enthusiasm and also co-operating in the artillery programmes with their 105-millimetre tank guns. Towards the end of January the Regiment was ordered to relieve 1st R.H.A. near Villanova and went under command 1st Canadian Division. Batteries remained in the same area for about seven weeks. They devoted much time to road making, for the continual rain and movement had ruined the indifferent roads, some of which had a coating of mud two feet deep. The general practice was to have one Battery forward at Villanova as a firing battery in turn.

## 2. Conquest in Italy

AT THE END OF 1944 there had been many changes in personnel and an influx of ex-A.-A. officers. Major Morris became second in command in succession to Major Richmond, who went back to United Kingdom just before Christmas. Major Dudley Smith and Major Charles left for United Kingdom in the New Year. The three Batteries at Villanova were then commanded: "A" by myself, "B" Major Parker and "E" Major Mansel. Capt. Thomson-Glover was appointed Adjutant.

During the relatively quiet period in the Villanova sector the Regiment was under command 1st Canadian Infantry Division, 2nd Armoured Brigade and 8th Indian Division and also supported the newly arrived Jewish Brigade and then Cremona Group. Towards the end of February and in March the Battery Commanders and Troop Commanders made many visits to the Forli area, where their armoured regiments, taken out to rest and train, were practising operations with Kangaroo-borne infantry of 78th Division. The infantry, particularly the Irish Brigade, soon became adept at movement and development from Kangaroos—the code word for a Priest, with the gun removed, used as an infantry carrier in close support of tanks. The Regiment completed absolute calibration of troop standard guns at Bellaria and a comparative calibration by firing into Lake Comachio.

Prior to the major assault on the Senio Line, the first move was to the extreme right, under command 56th Division, to support the 2nd Commando's amphibious assault on the Spit. " B " Battery sent O.P.s with 10th Hussars to support 56th Division, having arranged to fire 65th and 24th Field Regiments. The Regiment penetrated halfway up the Spit, then wheeled back to prepared positions to support the initial crossing of the Reno by 56th Division south-west of Lake Comachio. The Sextons were then ordered round to support the major crossing by the New Zealanders. Dummy Sextons and other camouflage were left in the gun positions on the right.

In the night 6th/7th April Batteries occupied forward positions near Cotignola on 78th Divisional front, ready to support the New Zealanders. The enemy fired a heavy counter-battery programme, " Leonidas," but the occupation was completed without casualties although some ammunition dumps were set on fire. Neither were there any casualties from machine-gunning or from the mines which were encountered in considerable quantities. The C.O. and Battery Commanders attended the New Zealand conference when General Freyberg gave details of the overpowering attack by aeroplanes, guns, tanks, flame-throwers and infantry which was scheduled to breach the Senio.

On " D " Day, 9th April, the gunners watched successive waves of heavy bombers and fighter-bombers fly over and then began their own contribution to the nine hour gun attack in which they fired over 13,000 rounds. Next day the Batteries closed up to the Senio and on the 11th moved to Lugo to marry up with 2nd Armoured Brigade. " E " Battery joined the group of 9th Lancers and London Irish Rifles mounted in Kangaroos, remaining on wheels ready to pass through in support of any breakout. " B " Battery's O.P.s were still with 10th Hussars, advancing east-west between the Lake and the River Reno. "A" and " B " Batteries concentrated with 2nd Armoured Brigade, "A" Battery's O.P.s joining The Bays in direct support of 38th Brigade group. Just before last light on the 12th The Bays crossed the Santerno and extended the bridgehead to a depth of 2,000 yards. The attack was now going well everywhere, with the New Zealanders pushing ahead on the left.

Before dawn the next day "A" Battery moved to a position just short of the Santerno and at first light 2nd Armoured Brigade group with " E " Battery crossed the Santerno, followed by " B " and then "A." The Bays with 38th Brigade turned north and advanced all day against opposition from self-propelled guns and infantry. Several smoke screens and fire plans were fired. The Kangaroo force was passed through and by 14th April the London Irish Rifles had exploited to the River Reno, indeed, established a small bridgehead until they were counter-attacked. " B " Battery's O.P.s were getting nearer and passed useful information of 56th Division moving to converge with 78th Division near Bastia, the entrance to the Argenta Gap. On 14th April " B " Battery O.P.s began to shoot their own Battery again at an apex angle of about 140 degrees.

On the following day the Regiment took on another commission, firing a five hour's barrage in support of 56th Division, what time The Bays, with "A" Battery O.P.s doubled back to cross the Reno in 56th Divisional area and came up once more towards Bastia on the north of the river with 11th Brigade. Traffic was very congested in the rush for the Argenta Gap, but friendly 5th Corps Provost gave the Sextons priority, doublebanked them through and over the Reno to positions south-east of Argenta.

Heavy dumping programmes were continually required and the Battery echelons, with 925th Company, Royal Army Service Corps, had scarcely an hour's rest ferrying ammunition to keep up with the advance. The echelon system worked so efficiently that the Regiment never had to touch first line supplies for all the barrages it was called upon to fire.

On the 17th April, the advance was speeded up with 10th Hussars on the right and The Bays on the left. Smoke screens were so popular with the armoured regiments that 10th Hussars asked for 16 Oboe screens to be on call. In the afternoon a squadron of The Bays crossed a canal by arc bridge and worked round behind Argenta to cut Route 16, with the result that the Regiment was called upon to cover a frontage of nearly 270 degrees. The battle was obviously developing into a considerable victory, for columns of German infantry were captured and marched back to the rear. The Germans fought tenaciously even when armour had overrun their positions, snipers were left behind to harass echelons and on one occasion a set-piece company attack was made to dislodge determined enemy infantry near 36th Brigade Tactical Headquarters. Snipers were very troublesome on Route 16, but the armourplate on the Sextons again proved its worth and there was only one casualty from sniping throughout the whole operation.

With 9th Lancers and the Kangaroo infantry leading, 2nd Armoured Brigade group were unleashed north of Argenta and raced forward to break through the gap. At nightfall on the 18th April, "A" and " E " Batteries were in action some miles ahead of the main body in support of the enterprising 9th Lancers' force.

The London Irish Rifles and 56th Reconnaissance, with " B " Battery O.P., made a bridgehead over the Porto di Fosso on 19th April. The Bays, with 11th Brigade, enlarged the bridgehead against strong opposition. The tempo speeded up once more on 21st April when 10th Hussars, who had rejoined 2nd Armoured Brigade, supported an attack by 38th Brigade. The 9th Lancers' group passed through and brushing aside resistance raced northwards to capture the Cona bridge intact. Batteries had been leapfrogged by the C.O. and, just before last light, once more formed a regimental area, the only guns within range of the battle.

Early next morning "A" and " B " Batteries both engaged the Po crossings. The Bays, with 11th Brigade, were sent to exploit from the Cona bridge and on the right a bridgehead was formed over the Po di Vollano. When this bridgehead was developed the whole Division switched right-handed and advanced to Tamara. Some counter-battery fire fell in the gun areas and it was clear the enemy was trying to keep open the Po crossing at Pollesella with a strong anti-tank gun screen and mobile S.P. guns.

In the afternoon of 24th April the axis of advance was switched to the south-west and 9th Lancers' group directed west on Ferrara. The advance pressed forward rapidly and 10 Mark IVs. were knocked out. Batteries were firing heavily in support of their regiments and many targets were seen and engaged as enemy transport reached the Po. That night everybody surged forward and the rout of the German forces south of the Po was complete. During darkness the last remnants of the enemy were thrown back to the Po where huge concentrations of M.T. and equipment were abandoned. Such destruction as at Zocca was certain proof of the utter defeat suffered by the Germans. Capt. Young, with " B " Squadron of The Bays, reached a viewpoint at Borgo on the morning of the 25th April and fired on observed targets across the Po.

During the final battle, from the Commando attack on the Spit to the Po, the Regiment had fired over 42,000 rounds of H.E. and some 4,500 rounds of smoke. The last round fired by "A" Battery across the Po on the morning of 25th April was the last fired by the Regiment in the war against Germany.

At 10.30 hours Regimental Headquarters ordered "Cease fire." Later that day the Regiment concentrated near Baura, hoping to cross the Po. Batteries remained on short notice to move and were disappointed when they were not allowed to continue the chase across the river to overrun the plain of Lombardy.

The Regiment expanded into more comfortable billets south of Ferrara and there celebrated first the victory in Italy and a few days later, on 8th May, victory in Europe. Regimental and Brigade church services, a sports meeting and other events were organised.

The Eighth Army moved steadily north, and on the week-end of 19th/20th May the Regiment was ordered to cross the Po and march north, skirting Venice to the Palmanova area. "B" Battery had left a week or so earlier to join 10th Hussars with 56th Division near the River Isonzo.

On arrival at Palmanova on 24th May "A" Battery was sent with a squadron of The Bays over the river to Skrbina some 20 miles north of Trieste. "B" Battery with 10th Hussars moved forward to positions near Comeno. There the Batteries remained with their armoured regiments while negotiations were proceeding with the Yugoslav forces to settle the difficulties which had arisen in the occupation of Carinthia and Trieste.

Demobilisation schemes, reduction in Python, overseas service and extended leave to United Kingdom were introduced. Underneath all these discussions there was an uneasy feeling that the Regiment might find itself in the melting pot—and a fervent hope that after so much, perhaps, at any rate the 200 odd originals might be allowed to go home as the 11th (H.A.C.) Regiment, R.H.A.

★   ★   ★

# APPENDIX

# Roll of Honour

*Officers Killed in Action :*

| | |
|---|---|
| Agheila | Lieut. J. L. F. Armitage |
| | 2/Lieut. H. F. C. Tompson |
| | 2/Lieut. W. M. Hart |
| "H" Tp. action | Lieut. J. W. Venning |
| Knightsbridge | Major J. R. O. Charlton, M.C. |
| | Major H. Bourne |
| | Major J. W. Hopkins, M.C. |
| | Lieut. M. V. Boys (died of wounds) |
| | Lieut. A. F. Worthington |
| | 2/Lieut. C. G. A. Leechman (died of wounds) |
| | 2/Lieut. F. C. Haldin |
| | 2/Lieut. R. Leftwich |
| | 2/Lieut. R. H. McDonald |
| Alamein | Capt. S. A. G. Watt |
| Tunisia | Capt. T. F. Butler-Stoney, M.C. |
| | Lieut. B. H. S. Laskey |
| | Lieut. A. S. Humphries (died of wounds) |
| Sicily | Major D. Rowlandson |
| | Capt. J. H. McAllum, M.C. (died of wounds) |
| Gothic Line | Capt. L. Q. Drage, M.C. |
| | Capt. A. W. Grant |

*Other Ranks Killed in Action :*

| | |
|---|---|
| Agheila | L/Bdr. Colwell, G. (died of wounds) |
| | Sigmn. Dorney, E. J. |
| | Gnr. Godfrey, D. |
| | Gnr. Grindey, D. (died of wounds) |
| | L/Sgt. Harold, H. J. (died of wounds) |
| | Gnr. Hill, E. L. K. |
| | Gnr. Hughes, W. E. (died of wounds) |
| | Gnr. Lewis, O. G. |
| | Gnr. Shea, A. |
| | Sgt. Town, M. J. T. |
| | Gnr. R. A. G. Steels, |
| "H" Tp. action | Sgt. Banbury, V. B. M. |
| | Gnr. Brazington, H. F. |
| | L/Bdr. Buckland, V. C. |
| | Gnr. House, H. L. V. |
| | Gnr. Lloyd, T. |
| | Gnr. Russell, A. H. |
| | Sgt. Steventon, J. E. |
| | Gnr. Sheldon, L. |
| Pre-Knightsbridge | Gnr. Hughes, A. T. (enemy air attack) |

Knightsbridge    ..    Gnr. ALLAN, G. I.
L/Bdr. BEST, R.
Bdr. BROWN, C. P.
Gnr. BAKER, S. (died of wounds)
Gnr. BARKER, L. (died of wounds)
Gnr. BALDING, E. G. (died of wounds)
Bdr. BOARDMAN, W. J. R. (died of wounds)
Gnr. CHAPPELL, A. K.
Bdr. CLARK, G. H. (died of wounds)
L/Bdr. COOK, H.
Gnr. CROWE, A. J.
L/Bdr. CRUTCHLEY, H. D.
Gnr. CONWAY, E. J. (died of wounds)
Gnr. CHAYTERS, H. (died of wounds)
L/Sgt. CALLAGHAN, L. R.
L/Sgt. DANDO, G. R.
L/Bdr. DAVIES, C. M.
Sgt. DEAKIN, J. W.
Gnr. DODD, G. J.
Bdr. DONALDSON, N. S.
Bdr. FARQUHAR, A. W.
Gnr. FLETCHER, G. W.
Gnr. GOLTENBOTH, G.
Gnr. GRIFFITHS, D. W.
S/Sgt. GOODMAN, A.
Gnr. HAYWOOD, C. F.
Gnr. HELM, C.
Bdr. HOLCROFT, E. C.
Gnr. HINGLEY, J. (died of wounds)
Gnr. HODGE, F. A. (died of wounds)
Bdr. HEYWARD, J. E.
Gnr. HILLS, T. (died of wounds)
Gnr. HOBSON, E.
Bdr. IRONTON, F. J. (died of wounds)
Gnr. JONES G. A.
Gnr. JONES, L.
Gnr. JONES, R.
Gnr. JEFFREYS, H. A.
Gnr. KNIGHT, F.
Bdr. LAWLEY, G. J.
L/Sgt. MADDOX, D.
Gnr. MANN, F. J.
Sgt. NICHOLL, G. M.
Bdr. NUNN, L. J.
L/Bdr. NOBLE, H. J.
Gnr. O'NEILL, G. L.
Gnr. PRATCHETT, A. L.
Gnr. RADLEY, S. J.
Sgt. ROWNTREE, W. H.
Gnr. ROGERS, C.
L/Sgt. RISHTON, N. (died of wounds)
Sgt. SNEDDON, A. D.
Gnr. SMITH, J. C.
Bdr. SMITH, A. C.
L/Bdr. SPAULL, S. G.
Sgt. SWINGLER, R. B. (died of wounds)

| | |
|---|---|
| Knightsbridge (*contd.*) | L/Sgt. TERRY, G. (died of wounds) |
| | B.S.M. THORNE, J. H. |
| | Bdr. TINSLEY, J. C. (died of wounds) |
| | Sgt. TOMPKINSON, S. M. |
| | B.S.M. TROTMAN, S. A. J. |
| | Sgt. VILLETTE, J. W. (died of wounds) |
| | L/Bdr. WILLIAMS, J. H. |
| | Gnr. WAKELIN, F. |
| | Gnr. WILLIS, E. A. |
| | Sgt. WILTSHIRE, C. L. |
| | Gnr. WATTS, R. F. |
| | L/Bdr. WHITTINGHAM, M. |
| | Gnr. WEBB, J. T. (died of wounds) |
| Alamein .. .. | Sgt. BAIRD, J. E. |
| | Bdr. BACK, W. J. |
| | Gnr. COCKBURN, W. S. |
| | Gnr. GOLDSTON, J. |
| | L/Cpl. GLENNON, W. E. |
| | Bdr. JEFFRIES, G. C. (died of wounds) |
| | Gnr. MALCOLM, J. |
| | Gnr. ROGERS, E. W. |
| | Gnr. VINEY, L. |
| | Gnr. WALTON, W. G. |
| | Gnr. WHITE, F. W. |
| | L/Bdr. WILLIAMS, R. S., M. M. (died of wounds) |
| Tunisia .. .. | Gnr. BUSBY, F. |
| | L/Bdr. EDGE, C. |
| | Sgt. KETTLE, J. R. (att. 1st Corps) |
| | Gnr. SHAW, J. W. |
| | Gnr. SMITH, T. C. |
| | Bdr. WATSON, E. (died of wounds) |
| | Gnr. WILSON, F. B. |
| Sicily .. .. .. | Gnr. HARPER, R. |
| | Gnr. PRYKE, G. E. |
| | Gnr. PHILIP, A. A. (died of wounds) |
| | Gnr. RICHARDSON, G. W. |
| | Gnr. STANFORD, R. (died of wounds) |
| | Gnr. WOOKEY, F. (died of wounds) |
| Gothic Line .. .. | Gnr. HARTY, M. |
| | Gnr. HILLS, L. H. |
| | Gnr. HESLOP, W. E. |
| | Gnr. HARTLEY, R. |
| | L/Bdr. HOLLOWAY, W. T. |
| | Gnr. JENKINS, D. (died of wounds) |
| | Bdr. PENNINGTON, A. M. |
| | Sgt. SMITH, G. W. |
| | Bdr. WARD, H. L. G. |
| Senio to the Po .. | L/Bdr. DUCKWORTH, A. |
| | Gnr. MORRISON, W. |
| Lost at Sea as Prisoners of War .. | Gnr. BALE, C. W. |
| | Sgt. BATTLE, W. G. |
| | Dvr. BESTWICK, J. H. |
| | Gnr. BETTANY, J. |
| | Gnr. BIDDULPH, F. J. |
| | Gnr. BROWN, G. |

Lost at Sea as
Prisoners of War (*contd.*)    Bdr. CADMAN, E. F.
Sgt. CHAPLIN, A. F.
Gnr. CHARD, L. C.
Gnr. CHEESEMAN, F. W.
L/Sgt. DUMMOTT, B. F.
Gnr. EDGE, M. B.
L/Sgt. EDWARDS, B.
Gnr. ERRY, N. W.
Sgt. FARRELL, P. E.
Gnr. FINBURY, J.
Gnr. GIBSON, R.
L/Sgt. GODDEN, A. H.
L/Bdr. GREEN, J. M.
Gnr. GRODEN, A.
Gnr. HATLEY, J. E. S.
Gnr. HAYES, E. N.
Gnr. HENNESSEY, A. V.
Gnr. HOPTON, J. E.
Gnr. HURLEY, T. W.
Gnr. JACKSON, P. D.
Gnr. JONES, D. M.
Gnr. LANE, L.
Gnr. LARNER, M. J.
L/Bdr. LEMON, C. S.
L/Bdr. McGRATH, G. B.
Gnr. MILLS, J. G.
Gnr. MUNRO, A. C.
B.Q.M.S. MURRAY, H. A.
Gnr. NYE, E. W.
Gnr. NYE, F. J.
Gnr. O'BRIEN, J. E.
Gnr. OSBORN, D. A.
Gnr. PEARMAN, T. E.
Gnr. PROSSER, J. J.
Gnr. RANGECROFT, W.
Gnr. SEEL, J.
Gnr. SIMMONS, H. D.
Gnr. SIMS, F.
Gnr. SMITH, T.
Gnr. SNELLING, G. W.
Gnr. STONE, E. L.
Gnr. STRETCH, A. A. H.
Gnr. TURNER, J. A.
Gnr. WILLINGHAN, C. L.
Gnr. WILSON, C. W.
Gnr. WORCESTER, G.
Gnr. WRIGHT, H. P.

Died as Prisoners of War    ..    ..    Gnr. COLE, J. A.
Gnr. CORDEN, S.
Gnr. GRIFFITHS, J.
Gnr. McCRACKEN, J.
Gnr. MAIR, G.
Gnr. MOXON, E.
Sgt. STRAITON, A.

Killed on Active
  Service       ..    ..   Gnr. Dorell, H. I.
                           Gnr. Robinson, E. W., M.M.
                           Sgt. Wright, H. B.
                           Gnr. Rooney, W.

## Honours and Awards

The following decorations have been conferred on personnel serving with the Regiment :—

D.S.O.        ..    ..    ..   Lieut.-Col. R. W. Goodbody
                               Lieut.-Col. W. M. Leggatt
                               Major J. R. Richmond, T.D.
Bar to M.C... ..    ..    ..   Major D. Morris, M.C.
                               Capt. J. W. Hopkins, M.C.
                               Capt. R. N. Smith, M.C.
M.C.          ..    ..    ..   Major J. P. Sworder
                               Major G. R. Armstrong
                               Major F. B. S. MacLaren
                               Major D. Morris
                               Major J. P. Charles
                               Capt. T. F. Butler-Stoney
                               Capt. G. N. Chastel de Boinville
                               Capt. R. N. Smith
                               Capt. E. Dudley Smith
                               Capt. K. E. Bolton
                               Capt. J. H. MacAllum
                               Capt. L. Q. Drage
                               Capt. J. S. Martin (R.A.M.C.)
                               Capt. J. D. Henderson
                               Capt. J. M. Page
                               Lieut. J. P. Thomson-Glover
G.M.          ..    ..    ..   Lieut. G. F. Moore
                               Gnr. Waters, J.
M.B.E.        ..    ..    ..   R.Q.M.S. Singleton, J.
D.C.M.        ..    ..    ..   L/Sgt. Dornton-Duff, C.B., M.M
                               Gnr. Simpson, D. B.
M.M.          ..    ..    ..   Sgt. Town, M. J. T.
                               Sgt. Knight, G. T. A.
                               Sgt. Kirk, S. F.
                               Sgt. Quinney, V. H.
                               L/Sgt. Dornton-Duff, C. B.
                               L/Sgt. Tomlin, D.
                               Bdr. Gilbert, F.
                               Bdr. Williams, R. S.
                               Bdr. Boardman, W. J. R.
                               Bdr. Parry, H. R.
                               Bdr. Bennett, P.
                               L/Bdr. Simmonds, H. D.
                               L/Cpl. Morans, J. (R.Sigs.)
                               L/Cpl. Holder, J. M. (R.Sigs.)
                               Gnr. Westwood, S. R.
                               Gnr. Robinson, E. W.

| | | |
|---|---|---|
| U.S.A. War Department—<br>Bronze Star | .. .. | B.S.M. FLUTTER, G. W. |
| Commendation Cards | .. | Major J. MCDERMID<br>Capt. J. V. C. PEARSON<br>Capt. K. E. BOLTON<br>Capt. R. N. SMITH |
| Mentions in Despatches | .. | Capt. R. W. DUNN<br>Capt. K. E. BOLTON<br>Capt. J. V. C. PEARSON<br>Lieut. R. M. FUNNELL<br>B.S.M. N. HODGSON<br>B.S.M. R. POPE<br>Sgt. SIMPSON, H. C. E.<br>L/Bdr. DEDMAN, A. M.<br>L/Bdr. FORSTER, A. P.<br>L/Bdr. COWEN, A.<br>Gnr. DAY, A. W.<br>Sigmn. ARCHER, L. M. R. (R.Sigs.)<br>Sigmn. DERRETT, R. F. (R.Sigs.)<br>Dvr. HODGSON, J. (R.A.S.C.)<br>Pte. READ, C. (R.A.M.C.) |

★ ★ ★

# Commands in which the Regiment has Served

1 Armoured Division
6 Armoured Division
7 Armoured Division
4 Infantry Division
46 Infantry Division
50 (Northumbrian) Division
51 (Highland) Division
56 (London) Infantry Division
78 Infantry Division
1 Canadian Infantry Division
8 Indian Division
2 Armoured Brigade
23 Armoured Brigade
Jewish Brigade

# Command and Appointments

During the period September 1939 until May 1945 the following Officers have held appointments in the Regiment as shown.

*Commanding Officer :*

Lieut.-Col. E. W. GOLDSWORTHY, T.D.
Lieut.-Col. W. A. EBBELS, M.C.
Lieut.-Col. G. B. VAUGHAN-HUGHES, M.C.
Lieut.-Col. W. M. LEGGATT, D.S.O.
Lieut.-Col. R. W. GOODBODY, D.S.O.
Lieut.-Col. J. H. SLADE-POWELL

| "A" Bty. | "B" Bty. |
|---|---|
| Major J. McDermid | Major P. Pettit |
| Major J. F. Adye | Major W. A. Sheil |
| Major G. R. Armstrong, M.C. | Major J. R. E. Benson |
| Major P. J. A. Hankey | Major J. E. F. Linton |
| Major L. Chrimes | Major J. P. Sworder, M.C. |
| Major E. Dudley Smith, M.C. | Major J. W. Hopkins, M.C. |
| Major K. E. Bolton, M.C. | Major F. B. S. MacLaren, M.C. |
| | Major D. Rowlandson |
| | Major J. P. Charles, M.C. |
| | Major J. G. Parker |

| "E" Bty. | *Adjutant :* |
|---|---|
| Major F. W. Gore | Capt. R. W. Goodbody |
| Major R. C. Croxton | Capt. J. P. Sworder |
| Major T. F. Butler-Stoney, M.C. | Capt. A. E. C. Green |
| Major D. Morris, M.C. | Capt. M. W. G. Wathen |
| Major E. C. Mansel | Capt. L. Q. Drage, M.C. |
| | Capt. K. E. Bolton, M.C. |
| | Capt. J. P. Thomson-Glover, M.C. |

★ ★ ★

## Summary of Battle Casualties—December, 1941 to May, 1945

|  | Killed in action or Died of Wounds | | Wounded in action | | P.o.W. | | Missing | | Wounded not evacuated | | Total | |
|---|---|---|---|---|---|---|---|---|---|---|---|---|
|  | Off. | Ors. | Off. | Ors. | Off. | Ors. | Off. | Ors. | Off. | Ors. | Off. | Ors. |
| Agheila | 3 | 10 | 2 | 13 | 3 | 75 | — | 4 | 2 | — | 10 | 102 |
| "H" Tp. action | 1 | 8 | — | — | 1 | 18 | — | 1 | — | — | 2 | 27 |
| Welcol | — | — | — | 5 | — | — | — | — | — | — | — | 5 |
| Knightsbridge | 9 | 70 | 17 | 158 | 10 | 201 | — | 31 | 1 | 1 | 37 | 491 |
| Alamein | 1 | 12 | 8 | 87 | — | — | — | — | — | — | 9 | 99 |
| Tunisia | 3 | 7 | 6 | 38 | — | — | — | — | 1 | 4 | 10 | 49 |
| Sicily | 2 | 6 | — | 11 | — | — | — | — | — | 7 | 2 | 24 |
| Gothic Line | 2 | 9 | 5 | 28 | — | — | — | 1 | — | — | 7 | 38 |
| Senio to the Po | — | 2 | — | 5 | — | — | — | — | — | 1 | — | 8 |
| Lost at sea as P.o.W. | — | 53 | — | — | — | — | — | — | — | — | — | 53 |
| Died as P.o.W. | — | 7 | — | — | — | — | — | — | — | — | — | 7 |
| Killed on Active Service | — | 4 | — | — | — | — | — | — | — | — | — | 4 |
| Total | 21 | 103 | 38 | 345 | 14 | 294 | — | 37 | 4 | 13 | 77 | 792 |

www.ingramcontent.com/pod-product-compliance
Lightning Source LLC
Chambersburg PA
CBHW060926170426
43192CB00025B/2907